THI

THE HIDDEN ROMANCE

OF THE

NEW TESTAMENT

BY

JAMES ALEX. ROBERTSON, M.A., D.D.

PROFESSOR OF NEW TESTAMENT LANGUAGE, LITERATURE AND
THEOLOGY, UNITED FREE CHURCH COLLEGE, ABERDEEN;
AUTHOR OF "THE SPIRITUAL PILGRIMAGE OF JESUS," ETC.

THIRD IMPRESSION

LONDON
JAMES CLARKE & CO., LIMITED
13 & 14, FLEET STREET, E.C.4

CONTENTS

PREFACE

THROUGH the landscape of the New Testament runs a single highway—the King's Highway, where the light of the Holy Presence beats strong. Our unaccustomed eyes are dazzled sometimes by the splendour, and we welcome the invitation to travel now and then down the obscurer by-ways. Here the subdued light falls softly through the shadows, and we are able to see, by the wayside, the lowlier beauties to which the full glory blinds us. It helps to make the New Testament a more real book to us when we know more intimately some of the people whose lives and deeds give the documents body and form. To discover the homelier personal background out of which the New Testament sprang is to relate it more nearly to the life of our day. We win a closer fellowship with the mountain when we have explored the *flora* on its lower slopes. It is with some of these humble personal details of the men and women who shared the New Testament experience, that we are here concerned. We may without presumption claim that the subject of this book is an aspect of the Humanism of the New Testament.

The book does not by any means pretend to exhaust the Hidden Romance of the New Testament. And indeed many of the conjectures and theories here offered may seem to the reader to be propounded with a much more dogmatic assurance than the writer actually feels. At best only a high probability can be claimed for many of them. One unyieldingly hostile fact is sufficient to destroy a theory.   Often a great many friendly ones are needed to establish it. The most probable theory is that which explains the greatest number of the facts, and is contradicted by none of them. Throughout, the writer has sought to keep this principle in view. But two other principles have been followed in the working out of these narratives. One is that because a fact has become thickly encrusted with legend, it is no mark of a true scientific instinct to deny the fact, or dissolve *it* also into myth or legend. A good deal of the historical criticism of recent years is vitiated by a too facile tendency in this direction. Again, it is often a first principle of this type of criticism that truth must always be commonplace ; it cannot on any account be allowed to be stranger than fiction. We assert, on the contrary, that truth is nearly always stranger than fiction. Any life, even the humblest and obscurest life in the world, if written with sympathy and insight, would be as absorbing as the most enthralling romance.

> 'Tis fiction's, to dilute
> To plausibility
> *Our* novel ; when 'tis small enough
> To credit, 'tisn't true !

And any dullness that may be found on these pages must be set down to the failure of the writer, not to the commonplaceness of the tales. The most romantic story in the world is the romance of the Divine Grace. It is surely not incredible that the journey of that Divine Grace through the traffic-ways of humanity should lead us

> Through widening chambers of surprise to where
> Throbs rapture near an end that aye recedes,
> Because *His* touch is infinite, and lends
> A yonder to all ends.

CHAPTER I

The Man of Arimathæa

WILLIAM OF MALMESBURY, a careful English historian of the early days, has recorded the legend, preserved through the Middle Ages, that Christianity first came to England when Joseph of Arimathæa was sent by the Apostle Philip from Gaul. Bearing in his custody the Holy Grail, Joseph found in the swamps of Somerset a conspicuous Tor that had a startling resemblance to Mount Tabor in the Holy Land. There he hid the Grail, and built the first Christian sanctuary in these islands of ours, in 63 A.D. It is here in this legend " all covered over with a luminous mist " that the Gospel story reaches out a long arm across the distance and makes contact with our land. There may be little of historical truth in the story, though there seems nothing intrinsically improbable in the suggestion that it was Joseph, or relatives of his, that brought the Gospel to England. The Grail is the symbol of the soul's holiest unsatisfied desire. And we place this legend in the forefront here as a symbol of the quest we have set ourselves—to explore, so far as it has been permitted to us, some chapters of the Hidden Romance of the New Testament.

A great Abbey was founded at Glastonbury, where the first Christian church was built, and it was a flourishing religious house in the days when the Crusaders set sail from England under Richard the Lion Heart. The tradition which had grown about the place had no doubt taken a deep hold on the religious mind of the day. And we can imagine the monks of Glastonbury laying a solemn charge upon the knights of the Red Cross to search for relics and recollections of their patron Joseph, when they reached the Holy Land. It is interesting to recall the fact that a large part of Richard's campaigning was undertaken towards Jerusalem, from the port of Jaffa as a base. And they would often traverse the region where Arimathæa lay.

But when the Crusaders returned to England, they had apparently nothing new to tell of Joseph. So for the most part the monks of Glastonbury had to be content with the apparently meagre details of the Gospel story. But were they so meagre after all ? We can picture these monks, going over all the details with loving care, to console themselves for their disappointment. And this would be something like the story that would unfold itself before them, concerning him whom they venerated as the founder of their Abbey—" Joseph, the man from Arimathæa."

It is by no means the rule to have names of places attached to the names of persons in the New Testament, and wherever it occurs there is some special significance. Joseph is always called " the man from Arimathæa," and his is almost the only case where the significance of the designation is obscure. Of course it means that Arimathæa was his home at one time or other. And while the probabilities are that it was his ancestral home, it is not impossible that he only settled there in the days beyond the Cross. It may have been to distinguish him from several other Josephs of note in the early Church—Joseph Barnabas, Joseph Barsabbas, or Justus—just as " Iscariot " distinguishes Judas from at least one other in the band of disciples. But why it should have been " of Arimathæa "—an insignificant place—rather than a cognomen such as " Barnabas," still remains obscure. Assuming for the moment that his family belonged to the place, it must have been a family of considerable social status in this " town of the twin hills." Wealthy, too, for Joseph was a man of wealth (Matt. xxvii. 57) ; and the Rabbi's profession was not lucrative. It was he who bought the fine linen grave-clothes in which Jesus' body was wrapped. And perhaps when he made his daring request of Pilate, he had to help the scornful, avaricious Roman to a favourable answer, with a sum of gold. He seems to have owned a piece of land in the outskirts of Jerusalem, beyond the Damascus Gate. It sheltered under the green knoll with its craggy out-cropping of rock which gave it the shape and name of " Skull "—Golgotha. " Now in the place where (Jesus) was crucified there was a garden, and in the garden a new-made sepulchre, wherein never man was yet laid." Joseph had probably hewn that tomb out of the rock, to be his own last resting-place some day. It was honoured by another Guest. " There laid they therefore Jesus." But we are hastening on too fast.

Joseph's parents had evidently means enough and ambition enough to give the boy a liberal education. They sent him to college or the House of the Midrash in Jerusalem. He had been a fine youth, mentally gifted, earnest-souled. Luke describes him in his later years: " a good man and a just "— not only a pious observer of the Law, but a man of lofty character. These two things did not always go together. Many a Pharisee, as Jesus' words about them indicate, was a pedantically scrupulous observer of all the fine points of the Law, but — a whited sepulchre. Joseph's ability is borne testimony to by the fact that he became a Rabbi; and so conspicuous did he become among his fellows that he was in due course elected to the Sanhedrin. He became a councillor, one of the Seventy who not only interpreted but administered the Law. In Judaism at its hey-day, and even under the rule of the Romans, education, politics and religion merged into one another. Education was the study of the Law of Moses: the Law of Moses was the Law of the land: and the observance of the Law was religion. The supreme ambition of the Jew was to become one of the Seventy. We might almost say it meant becoming a college professor, an ecclesiastical leader, and a member of Parliament—or at any rate of the Judicature—all in one. Joseph had reached that coveted position. Mark says he was an " honourable councillor "—a front-bench man, as we might say. And his chief friend in the Council Chamber was Nicodemus, who was a ruler of the Jews—one of the four chief men of the Sanhedrin—one of the Cabinet. These two men, to their everlasting honour, refused to vote with the Council on the momentous occasion when they condemned Jesus to death. Nicodemus protested indeed. Perhaps Joseph, a more youthful councillor, contented himself with silent support.

How was it that Joseph was led to take up this position in the trial of Jesus ? The Gospel furnishes us with a considerable part of the answer. For Luke further describes Joseph as one " who also himself waited for the Kingdom of God." Now that is a phrase laden with a touching significance. We find it, or words to the same purpose, more than once in the Gospel story. There is Simeon, " who was waiting for the consolation of Israel (Lk. ii. 25), Anna, who belonged to a circle who " looked for redemption in Jerusalem " (Lk. ii. 38), the two on the road to Emmaus, who had been expecting Him " that should redeem Israel " ; blameless people like Zacharias and Elizabeth (Lk. i. 6), and others. In short, Joseph of Arimathæa, and doubtless his family, belonged to that religious class in Israel, known as the Chasidim. The Chasidim are not a sect, not an organised society. What they represent is a phase of religion which repeats itself in the religious life of almost every land. They are the devout people, simple, earnest, wistfully expectant, praying people, " the quiet in the land," hidden away often in the hills and the glens ; the people who keep the light of real, experimental religion burning through long dry times in the religious history of a nation.

There is almost a perfect parallel in the history of Scotland. During the long twilight of Moderatism which followed the Settlement after the Covenanting days, there sprang up spontaneously, often in remote districts, all over Scotland, what were known as praying circles. People " waiting for the consolation of Israel," we might with perfect aptness describe them. They met in each other's houses. They had no recognised leaders, no programme. But after the day's work, they might be seen straggling in twos or threes along hill-paths, by the side of the burn, or through the woods, as the gloaming gathered quickly, all making for a light that burned brightly in a little cottage window up the glen. They entered the house quietly, hardly even exchanged greeting, spent the evening in praise and prayer and meditation on God's word. And then at the end of the evening, shook hands silently and stole away. Out of these circles came the movements of Secession and Relief, and then the evangelical movement which ended in the Disruption. In the Highlands it took a special aspect, which manifested itself at communion seasons in a body known as "the Men". In its earlier stages, these "Men" were just the bright stars of the Chasidim, the pious in the land. In its later stages, they came to bear a grotesque similarity to an outgrowth of Israel's Chasidim—the Pharisees. "The Men" sometimes became proud, rigid, censorious, self-styled leaders of religion.

Joseph of Arimathæa was brought up in that circle at its best, devout, warm, tender, eagerly waiting people. It is said that only those were admitted into their circle who were cultured—well versed in the sacred Law,—and whose youth had never been defiled by sin. This religious upbringing was doubtless the secret of the youth's eagerly enquiring mind, which had led him at College to probe so deeply into his people's Faith ; he was waiting for the Kingdom—not in the sense in which people were commonly expecting it, not as a great political uprising, a successful revolt against the powers that be ; nor yet as a spectacular intervention of God—a coming in the clouds of heaven, such as another fanatical sect were expecting. He was looking for a quickening of real religion once more in Israel, a time of refreshing, a sound of abundance of rain, a blowing of the breath of the Spirit on the dry bones of the dead formalism of the time, a

14

restoring of the old songs to Sion—laughter and singing and joy, because God had visited His people.

He and his friend Nicodemus must have gone to Jordan to see the great religious revival there under John the Baptiser. And their unrest, their eager waiting, must have grown well-nigh unbearable —until they met Christ at length, and knew in their heart of hearts that what they had longed for was come. There was an air of mingled strangeness, beauty, and fear about this sublimely lowly Man— so simple, so inexorable in His demands upon the soul. And the experience created a terrible problem for these two men. To come out suddenly and decidedly and openly on the side of the Nazarene meant for both of them the most tremendous sacrifice that life could demand of them. It meant renouncing their calling, status, fame, the highest posts of public honour in the land. Jesus had won them—it was only a matter of time. But for long that inward strife and anguish of soul raged in Joseph's bosom. For of this too we have proof. He was, says Matthew, "a disciple of Jesus"; and the Fourth Evangelist adds the one phrase sadly qualifying that description—"but secretly for fear of the Jews."

The crisis came at last—and the victory. Perhaps it was in the very hour when Jesus was hanging on the Cross. Certainly a few hours later, Joseph's decision was made. Perhaps he was an onlooker, watching from the privacy of his garden, when the Great Tragedy was being enacted on the rocky knoll above. Trembling with excitement he must have passed the hours. It was the end of Jesus. To all human appearance the Cause was lost, the Nazarene discredited for ever and ever. His followers were scattered and fled. Yet it was then that he decided to offer his own tomb, that the body might be reverently interred. Probably it was later—on the road to Emmaus, some have thought—that the light broke, and he said to himself, " Jesus is the Redeemer, the Suffering Servant of God, dying for the sin of many, dying for my craven-heartedness. Here I make an end for ever of all my hankering after pride of place and power. My lectures in the House of the Midrash, my seat in the Council, my authority among the citizens of Jerusalem—I fling them all over ; I offer them as a humble sacrifice to Thee, who hast made the last great sacrifice for me."

And next we see him standing before Pilate with pale but resolute face, begging the despised and execrated body—begging it " with tears and entreat-ties," says the writer of the *Acts of Pilate*. And then in the waning light of day, he and his friend and some women assistants find their way back to Calvary, just as the soldiers are finishing their ghastly work, and smashing the legs of the criminals. We know of few more extraordinary, more moving scenes in history than this—two of the proudest in the land breaking the Law of which they were accredited and venerable teachers and administrators, making themselves unclean, putting themselves without the pale, in order to perform the last sad and tender offices of love and reverence for an Out-cast, who had died a felon's death. Daring death themselves—and they knew it. In the *Acts of Pilate* and *The Narrative of Joseph*, is it not recorded that Joseph was actually imprisoned by his enraged fellow-councillors, with a view to his execution ? But Pilate had had enough of blood and Joseph was released.

* * * *

The Man of Arimathæa

Such is the story from the Gospel pages, with which the disappointed monks of Glastonbury would comfort themselves, when the Crusaders returned bearing no relics or traditions about the great founder of their Abbey, to delight their hearts. And we would turn back now for a moment from following the fortunes of Joseph of Arimathæa, to join the company in Glastonbury Abbey once again. When the monks had consoled themselves in some such way as we have suggested, they must have begun to recall a story which the Crusaders had told them, and put a great deal of excitement and enthusiasm into the telling. It was a story to which the soldiers of Richard had listened many a time when they lay in the tented fields round Lydda, the little town a few miles inland from the port of Joppa, where their great commander had his headquarters. And this is how it goes.

About the year 303 A.D., when the Roman Emperor Diocletian issued his edict, ordering all the Christian churches to be burned, and their sacred books to be destroyed, a military tribune named Georgios, a man of good birth, a Christian, tore down the edict and suffered the penalty of death in consequence.

It was the eve of the triumph of Christianity. And the prevailing tradition points to the town of Lydda, as the place where the deed was wrought. It is not far from the reputed site where — in the ancient myth—Perseus slew the dragon and rescued Andromeda. It was natural that the soldier Georgios should come to be known as the slayer of the dragon of Paganism ; one of the champions to whose martyr blood the victory of " the Galilean " is due. The Crusaders told the story, and said that

on one occasion they were saved from disaster by
the intervention of this martyr saint. By-and-by
the story became so familiar and popular, that
it was only a step to making him the patron
saint of England—St. George, who slew the
dragon.

We can imagine the monks of Glastonbury turning
this story over in their minds, in the dim hope that
they might be able to connect it with their own.
It is certain that the two stories reached the zenith
of their vigour as a result of the Crusades. And it
is certain that the monks would begin to make eager
enquiries about this town of Lydda, which lay, as
they noted, not so many miles away from the reputed
site of Arimathæa. What is the history of this
town; and has the New Testament anything to say
about it?

Josephus, the Jewish historian, describes it as
" a village not less than a city." It lay on the
Eastern edge of the great plain of Sharon, near
where the foothills begin to rise towards the mountains of Judæa. It was a frontier town. The land
of Israel and the seaboard land of the Philistines,
Israel's hereditary enemies, met at this place. It
must have been in part an industrial town. The
region in which it lay was known as the Valley of
the Smiths—a fact reminiscent of the time when
Israel learned by bitter experience to grind her
own axes, and not to be dependent on her enemies
(1 Sam. xiii. 19). But it was also a flourishing
commercial town—a centre of the purple trade.
For it stood at a great cross-roads, where the
immemorial caravan route from Egypt to Damascus
and the East crossed the road from the port of Joppa
to the Jewish capital.

The Man of Arimathæa

It is easy to understand the strong nationalism of the citizens of this town. It was one of the hot-beds of revolution against the rule of Rome before the great outbreak which ended in the destruction of the Holy City. Its citizens had been sold into slavery in 44 B.C., for refusing to pay the Roman levies. They were liberated by Antony, but the memory rankled. It was burned by Cestius Gallus in the reign of Nero. It was captured by Vespasian in the year 68 A.D. It was natural that so patriotic a place should become one of the chief seats of the College of Rabbis, after the fall of Jerusalem.

To this day there is a Christian congregation at Lydda. The revolutionary Faith found a ready soil in the revolutionary town. The Christian community there seems to have made its influence felt in a very marked way on the life of the town—propagandists, zealous even to the point of fanaticism, proclaiming their message at the street-corners, on the house-tops, anywhere. There is one reluctant and curious testimony to the power of Christianity there. The Talmudists who settled in Lydda were irritated into making scornful reference to the sect. In the Talmud's careless and hazy allusion, Lydda is the place where the new sect sprang into being. It suggests that Lydda had been the home of Jesus and His mother Mary, upon whom it casts an unworthy aspersion. It says Lydda is the place where, " on the eve of Pascha " —a corroboration of the synoptic narrative—Jesus was condemned to death. The value of a report so malicious is that it proves the strength of the Christian community in Lydda at an early period of the Church's history. And probably the later references to the wretchedness and waywardness of Lydda are an indirect and spiteful tribute to the Church's ever-growing power. Lydda, in fact, seems to have become one of the main centres of Palestinian Christiani y. Even Mahomet is said to have prophesied that " Isa (Jesus) will slay Antichrist at the Gate of the Church of Lydda."

Now open the New Testament at the book of " the Acts," and you will find that there was a wide-spread accession to the Christian Faith when the Apostle Peter visited the town (Acts ix. 35). But you will find there also that it was not the Apostle who first proclaimed the Cross of Christ at Lydda. For Luke tells us that he came down on that occasion " to the saints which dwelt at Lydda." Who, then, was the Church's founder ? It may be that Philip the Evangelist had laboured there. But there is reason for believing that the Church in Lydda had an older origin still. Christ's first followers hailed from all parts of the Holy Land. We read of two in the Gospel story who had their home in Emmaus, not very far away. Tabitha, who lived a few miles further down in Joppa, is called a " disciple." And that probably means that she was one of the women followers of Jesus in the days of His flesh. And it is extremely likely that the wealthy Cypriote Mnason, who entertained Paul on his last momentous journey from Cæsarea to Jerusalem, had settled in Lydda. Luke calls him " a disciple of the beginning," and he probably means that Mnason had also been a follower of Jesus. Aeneas, whom Peter healed, was doubtless one of " the saints which dwelt at Lydda," and from the word which Peter spoke to him, it seems possible that he too had known the Prophet of Galilee.

The Man of Arimathæa

The monks in Glastonbury would ponder over all these things, until they suddenly realised that Arimathæa, the town of their own patron, lay not so far away. What if Joseph of Arimathæa had had something to do with the founding of the Church at Lydda ?

And with this surmisal in their minds they would go back to Joseph's story. Where would Joseph have gone, after that momentous day when he had resigned everything to follow Christ ? His old associates in the Sanhedrin would have made life intolerable for him in the ancient capital. Does not the very title by which he was always known in the early Church suggest that it was back to Arimathæa ? And surely a man who had made such a tremendous renunciation could not possibly have remained a mere passive disciple. We may be certain that he became an evangelist of flaming zeal. He must have wandered through all the region round Arimathæa telling his story. May not this be the explanation of the title which the early Christians always gave him ? He would be familiarly known by the Christians among whom he laboured as " the man from Arimathæa." And the busy little excitable town not so many miles away would not have been passed by. It cannot be thought incredible that this enthusiastic church may have owed its origin, under God's Spirit, to the great self-consecration of Joseph of Arimathæa. Nor yet that in later days he would have carried his evangelistic zeal into wider fields. It is at the instigation of Philip that he is said to have visited the Western lands of Europe. He may have passed through Rome and seen the aged Paul. Indeed, if Paul was liberated, and fulfilled his ambition to visit Spain, Joseph may have been in his company. It may have been to satisfy the longing of the frail, worn Apostle of the Gentiles that, if the tradition be correct, he crossed to Britain, carrying the Gospel to the " islands of the sea."

* * * *

How did he come to confess his allegiance to Christ ? How did he come to join himself to the disciples ? He was the man who buried the dead body of the Master; the man who associated himself with the ministering women in their last pious service for their Lord. He must have learned from them where the disciples were mourning, in the seclusion of the Upper Room—if, indeed, he had not known it before. Surely he must have sought them out now, to tell them what he had done, and to confess at last his long-hidden love for Jesus. Tender and sacred must the interview have been. His tale must have brought some consolation to the weeping disciples. And when they had heard him out and welcomed him to their company, he must have listened in his turn to the story they had to tell. Brokenly they must have recalled the memories of their Lord, until they came to the most recent and most intimate of them all—the memory of the Last Supper. Mingling again with their tears and sighs would come the great and wonderful words of love and sacrifice which their Lord had spoken at that table ; and then the story of the broken bread—the symbol of His body broken—and of the passing of the Cup of Communion, the Cup of blessing—the freely shared Forgiveness of God. That must have been the hour

The Man of Arimathæa

when the eyes of Joseph's heart began to grow clearer, and to behold in radiant and ecstatic vision the Divine meaning of it all.

Need we hesitate so very much to add one last touch to the picture ? " See," we fancy we hear the disciples saying to Joseph, " here is the Cup, the very Cup the Master sanctified to holiest service. It is for ever sacred to us, and we fear to lose it. Who should preserve it but thou, Joseph, who hast done the last reverence to the Master, washing the blood-stains from the broken body, ere thou didst lay it in thy grave ? "

The very Cup ! What a priceless treasure to possess ! " This cup," said Jesus, " is the new Covenant in my blood which is shed for many." To Joseph it must have been the thrice sacred memorial of the end of his long search for the Kingdom of Heaven, the vision of God ! That Cup is the Christian Holy Grail ! Buried in the soil of England, the ancient legend has it. Mingled and overlaid, indeed, with fragments of Celtic mythology, it has, nevertheless, become one of the most splendid symbols in all the noblest dreams of our country's literature, which is the voice of our country's soul. Sir Galahad, " the purest knight of Arthur's Table Round," made the search for it his life-long quest, and was granted at last to see it in sacramental vision. Fiction or fact, the story of this holy vessel stands there at the dawn of England's religious history, a sacred ideal, a dream that links our faith inseparably and immediately with the Cross. The story of Joseph of Arimathæa should always be to us a memorial and inspiration of the Beatific Vision which is granted to the pure in heart, a dream of splendour which we shall one day meet with face to face when we have purified ourselves even as Christ is pure.

Let it also be to us a symbol beckoning us in our adventure of exploration along the hidden ways that run through the land of the New Testament. And if we do not always reach a satisfying end to our quest, we may, like the Crusaders, bring back some fragments of the Church's early past, worthy to be set alongside the story of England's patron saint, St. George.

CHAPTER II

The House of the Upper Room

THE story of the Christian Church begins in the room of a private dwelling-house in Jerusalem. St. Cyril of Jerusalem, a fourth century writer, significantly names this little meeting-house " the *upper* church of the Apostles." A writer of a few years later informs us that it was the place where " the Lord came in to His disciples when the doors were shut," where also, on the day of Pentecost " the multitude were gathered together with the apostles "—a statement which is corroborated in the ancient Liturgy of St. James. Epiphanius mentions a tradition which goes back to the reign of Hadrian, to the effect that this " little church of God " was one of the few buildings left standing when Titus sacked the city in 70 A.D. A plan, dating apparently from the seventh century, and reproduced in the work *On Holy Places* by the Scottish Saint, Adamnan, identifies the site. Although the original building has long since disappeared, the house which now occupies the spot is known as the *cœnaculum*. " Of all the most sacred sites," says Dr. Sanday, " it is the one which has the strongest evidence in its favour. Indeed the evidence for it appears to me so strong that, for my part, I think I should be prepared to give it an unqualified adhesion."

Hidden Romance of the New Testament

Romance, which has a way of gathering about old houses, has nothing greater to show than that which gathers about this quiet home. What was the house ? To what house would the scattered disciples most naturally return, when they rallied after Calvary ? Would it not be to the house where they had held the last intimate intercourse with their Master before His death—the place where He told them He was about to be taken from them, and after the custom of the parting guest in Eastern lands, passed round the pledge-cup, saying, " This do in remembrance of me " ? Would it not be there, in their sorrow, that they would fondly recall the last tender utterances and, from the very cup He had shared with them, drink, in obedience to His last command ?

But is there any suggestion of this in the New Testament ? Let us listen first to the words of the Gospel narrative :

" The first day of unleavened bread—the day for killing the Paschal lamb—His disciples said to Him, ' Where do you want us to go and prepare for you to eat the Passover ? ' So He sent two of His disciples, telling them, ' Go into the city and you will meet a man carrying a water-jar : follow him, and whatever house he enters, tell the master of the house that the Rabbi is asking, Where is my room where I can eat the Passover with my disciples ? He will himself show you a large room upstairs, with couches spread ; there prepare for us the Passover.' The disciples went away into the city and found things just as He had told them. So they prepared the Passover, and when evening fell He arrived along with the Twelve. . . ."

Mystery greets us on the threshold. We see

two men coming in from the direction of Bethany along the road that winds round the shoulder of Olivet. They are talking together :

" Did He not say, Jochanan, a man with a water-jar, just inside the gate ? He must have arranged all this with one of the secret followers in the city. But why did He do it Himself so privily ? "

" I think I know, Simeon," his companion answers. " Did you not see how anxiously He looked at Judah before He gave us our instructions ? There is some weight upon His mind concerning Judah. I never liked the man. All is not well with him. I think I can guess, too, who the friend in the city is. But here is the Valley-gate. Let us enter and see."

* * *

The reason why Jesus wanted to eat this meal *within* the city is obvious. It was the Paschal meal, and the holy feast should be held within the holy city. If we accept the synoptic date for the meal —Thursday night of Passion Week—this may still hold good ; for it has been suggested that the twilight between the fourteenth and the fifteenth of Nisan fell that year on Sabbath eve, and since the killing of the Paschal lamb that evening would have been a violation of the Sabbath law, the Paschal meal in such a case was generally held the night before. But night-time in the city was fraught with danger for Jesus. And the precaution which He exercised is obvious. When the disciples were bidden to ask in their Master's name, " Where is *my* guest-chamber ? " we seem to have evidence that He had arranged before-hand with a friend. It is natural to expect that He would choose the house of a friend who resided on the edge of the city towards the hill of Olives where

He was to pass the night. Surely this is borne out by the nature of the preconcerted signal—the man with the water-jar. Ostensibly he was returning from the city-watering-place in Gihon. The house where the disciples met after the Crucifixion claims, therefore, for its site precisely that part of the city where we should expect to find the house of the Upper Room. Moreover, the place where they met is called an "upper" room. Luke, indeed calls it "*the* upper room"—an indication that it was familiarly known as such in the early Church, and in designating it so (Acts i. 13), Luke at the same time informs us it was the place "where the disciples were residing." The seclusion of the place—on the outskirts of the city—would attract them, too ; for they were afraid of the men who had crucified their Master, and met at first behind locked doors (John xx. 19).

Surely it is a sacred place in Christian history ; the scene of the Last Supper the night before the Cross ; the disciples' hiding-place after what must have seemed to them the great disaster ; the scene of their mourning ; the place where their sorrow gave way to a mysterious and startling sense that the Spirit of their crucified Lord was present—that His personality had victoriously survived the rude rending of the casket of the flesh ; the room to which they and other friends resorted for those days of intense and eager prayer ; the room where, after six or seven weeks, the Divine Spirit somehow rushed upon them, seized them, roused them to an extraordinary fervour and enthusiasm—the first appearance of that phenomenon which the Christian Church has grown familiar with in every great revival ; the birthplace of the Church of Christ.

The House of the Upper Room

It is into the hidden or obscure side of the fascinating story that our eager curiosity fain would penetrate. Perhaps nothing more than probability can be claimed for the tale that seems to unfold before our questioning. But it serves as an alluring starting-point from which to trace some further strands of the amazing story of the early days of the Gospel.

Who were the inmates of this house—these secret friends of Jesus in Jerusalem?

Let us follow the two disciples a little further, as they enter to prepare for the sacred meal. They pass through the Valley-gate at the south-west corner of the city-wall—the natural point of approach from the road along which they had come. And there was a man just lifting a water-jar to his shoulder. The man looked cautiously all round about him. Then he looked keenly at the two travellers. A gleam of intelligence appeared for a moment in his eyes. He placed his finger on his lips, and then turned his back on them, and went on before them, climbing up the steep way that ran north-east into the city. He had not gone very far before he turned down an unfrequented lane. He turned and looked at the two men for a moment, then passed in through a courtyard gate. John nodded to Peter. "It is even as I thought." They followed, gave the goodman of the house their message, and he conducted them in person to the room, where we leave them getting the place in order.

* * * *

All that we can gather out of the mystery that surrounds the house in this Gospel story is that there were at least two inmates, a male head, and either a son or a trusted slave who could be let in to share the secret. But in either case we may infer that there were women inmates also. We have to turn elsewhere for further light on the subject.

We have already noted that it was to "the upper room, where they were residing," that the disciples returned after the Ascension, "from the hill called the Olive-orchard"—a phrase which again suggests a house on the south side of the city. Is there any further reference to their lodging-place? We turn over a few pages of this narrative of Luke's. Peter has just escaped from Herod's prison. He suddenly finds himself in the street in the dead of night. "When he grasped the situation he went to the house of Mary, the mother of John, surnamed Mark, where a number had forgathered for prayer. When he knocked at the wicket in the gate, a girl-slave called Rhoda came forward to answer; but recognising Peter's voice, from sheer elation she neglected to open the wicket, but ran in and announced that Peter was standing there." Peter was soon in their midst, telling his story amid confused exclamations of joy. "Report all this," he said, "to James and his brothers." Then he withdrew and went to another place.

Again it is a house about which a certain air of mystery hangs. But certain inferences may easily be drawn from the story. Where would Peter turn when he was released from prison, but to the house of his most familiar friends? And why should he at once leave it when he had told his story, if not for the reason that this house would be suspect, a resort of the followers of the Nazarene, the house that would first be searched

The House of the Upper Room

when Peter's escape from prison was discovered. It was a house where the fortunes of the early Church in the holy city were a matter of intense concern ; it was a meeting-place of Christians, for a number had met, that anxious night, for prayer. More than that, the girl-slave at once recognised Peter's voice. Long familiarity had accustomed her to its tones. Nor would Peter have given them instructions to tell that other body of Christians who were by this time gathering round James and the other brothers of the Lord, unless he was certain they would be meeting with them next day. Here is, indeed, strong *prima facie* evidence that this is none other than the house of the Upper Room where the disciples had for a time been resident. But the evidence is stronger than that. We turn to the second last sentence of the first letter attributed to Peter : " My son Mark sends you greetings." Peter is writing from Rome (he calls it Babylon). Mark is helping to write down the letter from Peter's dictation. It is long years after those first exciting days in Jerusalem. But Mark, the son of the family with whom Peter was so well acquainted in those early days, has become the close companion and secretary of the great Apostle. Peter calls him " my son," and in the New Testament that is usually much more than a mark of affection, when it is used by one who is not related by blood. It indicates that Peter was the means of winning the young man to the side of the Nazarene. Paul often uses it in this sense.

Now the second Gospel is called the Gospel according to Mark. And we have evidence in the writings of the early Fathers that the writer was none other than this John Mark. " Mark," we are told, "having become the interpreter of Peter, wrote down accurately everything that he remembered, without however recording in order what was either said or done by Christ. For neither did he hear the Lord, nor did he follow Him. But afterwards . . . he attended Peter, who adapted his instructions to the needs (of his hearers), but had no design of giving a connected account of the Lord's words. So then Mark made no mistake while he thus wrote down some things as he remembered them, for he made it his one care not to omit anything that he heard, or to set down any false statement therein." These are the famous sentences which Eusebius quotes out of a book he possessed, written by a still older Church Father, Papias. And Papias says he heard the story from the lips of John the Elder, a follower of the early days—possibly the beloved disciple.

Our result then is that the family of the house of the Upper Room was the family of which John Mark was an inmate. It is no objection to point out that in the story of Peter's escape from prison, the house is called "the house of Mary, the mother of John, surnamed Mark"; for the death of the Apostle James, which immediately preceded Peter's imprisonment, took place more than a dozen years after the crucifixion. So that the "goodman of the house" mentioned in the Gospels, the husband, probably, of Mary, may have died before this time. It was evidently a family in comfortable circumstances and probably one of the many in the Holy City, like that of Joseph of Arimathæa, which belonged to the class of Chasidim, who had been "waiting for the consolation of Israel." It surely belongs to the fitness of things that one of the chief recorders of the immortal story should have been a son of the house of the Upper Room.

Mark's family was probably Hellenist-Jewish. They were connected with a family of Cypriote Jews. His Latin surname shows that he had intercourse with a circle wider than that of Judæa. He not only knew Aramaic, but could speak Greek; of this his position as interpreter to Peter assures us. He had had a good education, and could write. One or two touches in the Gospel narrative, peculiar to Mark (i. 36, xvi. 7, xiv. 37), besides the specific references to Peter which the other evangelists probably borrow from Mark, seem to indicate the influence of Peter in the telling of the story (cf. also xi. 21, xiii. 3). That the Gospel was written in Rome and for a Roman audience is supported by considerable internal evidence. Mark frequently explains Jewish words and customs (vii. 3f, 11, 34, iii. 17, v. 41, xv. 42), sometimes uses Latin words (v. 9, vi. 27, vii. 4, xv. 39), or Latin idioms (iii. 6, v. 23, xiv. 65, xv. 15), and explains Greek words by Latin equivalents (xii. 42, xv. 16), etc.

But, however interesting it might be to pursue these details, we turn away from the enticement to follow a hidden by-path of his story. We open his Gospel near the end. The scene is the Garden of Gethsemane. The rabble have just seized Jesus. And Mark writes, " Then they (the disciples) forsook Him and fled, all of them." It is the little incident which follows that excites our curiosity. "One young man had followed Him, with only a linen sheet thrown round his bare body. And they seized him. But he fled away naked, leaving the sheet behind him."

It is a vivid little story even though there cling about it some of the shadows of the Garden. What is its explanation? How comes it here? John Mark's Gospel is an outline of the story of Jesus pieced together as well as he could from the many addresses which he had listened to from the lips of Peter on his mission-tours. But we can be quite certain that Mark never heard Peter telling this incident. It sheds no light on the main theme. It does not help forward the narrative of the arrest. It has no bearing on the demeanour of Jesus. It would have no conceivable value in any possible address of Peter's. From the point of view of Peter the preacher, it would be an absolutely irrelevant detail. For us to-day, of course, far removed from the events and not in touch with eye-witnesses, the case is different. The incident enhances the actuality of the story, and we are grateful to the writer for inserting it. But for Peter, as he told the story of the great tragedy with burning passion, it would have been an insignificant and pointless side-issue. It seems merely to render the young man ridiculous; it adds an incongruous touch of comedy to the horror of the scene. That is one reason why we cannot think Mark got it from the lips of Peter.

But here is another. Mark has just said the incident took place a moment or two after the disciples had stampeded. Peter was by this time decamping in terror through the wood. Who would have reported this incident in after days? Not any of the disciples. Not any of that noisy and disordered rabble, enemies of the Lord. Only the young man himself, whose sympathies seem to have been on the side of Jesus, could have told it. Mark takes care to inform us in an emphatic phrase, the disciples had fled, " all of them."

Who then was he ? He was somebody, Mark says, who had followed Jesus—followed Him from the city to the Garden. And we remember that Jesus and the disciple-band had just celebrated the Paschal meal, all by themselves, secretly in the Upper Room of a friend's house on the edge of the city. When they left the house to go out to Gethsemane it was dark and late. They had only a few unfrequented by-streets to traverse ere they were beyond the walls. None of the usual followers could have joined them. This solitary youth must have been an inmate of the House of the Upper Room. But, further, none of the other evangelists thought it worth while telling the story but Mark. The inference is well nigh irresistible that this youth was John Mark himself. There is a tradition which says John Mark was known in the early Church as the " stump-fingered." Perhaps he had got the tips of some fingers shorn off by a sword-slash in the tussle, when he was forced to let go the sheet and flee naked. And when men asked about his stump-fingers this was the story he told.

There is something touchingly human in his thrusting it into the Gospel. It is " the signature of the artist in an obscure corner of the picture." It is as though he were saying : " On the scene of this tragic world-drama I myself appeared for an instant, and in one of its darkest hours. This is the point where I, a mere youth, first felt the breath of the Unseen touching me from this Life of lives." And when the readers of the Gospel asked him about it afterwards, we can see them in imagination listening to this tale :

" I was very curious about the strange party that met in our house that night. We had our own Paschal meal downstairs. Being the son of the house, I had to ask my father the questions of the rite. And I remember how excited my father was. There was a peculiar significance in his tones when he spoke about the promised Messiah ; he said He was here, and His hour was at hand. As usual on Paschal night, the door was open, and there was a special eagerness in my father's voice when he sent me to look for the sign of the great forerunner Elijah's return. He was evidently expecting him as he never expected him before. But the hours went by and nothing happened. He sent me to sleep on the terrace outside the door of the room above the gate, where the guests were feasting. He told me to extinguish the lights when the guests were gone ; and to watch and watch as long as wakefulness remained in my eyes. I spread my pallet near the door of the room and drew the cover over me. The feast of the strangers was protracted long after ours. I could hear the sweet, sad rise and fall of the Rabbi's voice—for so my father greeted Him. I had seen Him come in ; what a kind, sad face it was ! I was only a boy, and understood nothing of what it all meant ; but my heart was drawn to Him. I felt there was some dreadful sorrow hanging over Him. And all the early hours of the night I was excited and disturbed. I could not sleep. Then suddenly the door opened, and one solitary figure came out, loomed in the lighted doorway for a moment, and then he was alone in the dark ; the door was closed behind him. I watched his hesitating, uncertain movements as he slowly descended the stone steps. And he was muttering to himself. What it was I could not tell, but there was a sound as of cursing in it. I lay down on my couch again, and drew the sheet around me, for the night was chilly. But I could not sleep. I tossed and tossed. I was filled with a nameless fear about the Man with the sad, kind, noble, face. By-and-by I heard them singing the Hallel inside. Then the door opened once again. I saw the Rabbi thoughtfully extinguishing the lights as His followers left the room. And they all came out in silence and trooped down the steps in the dark. And a great pain came into my heart and I began to weep, I knew not why. The footsteps of the little company were dying away down the deserted street, when a sudden frenzy of desire took possession of me. I could not lie there any longer. I scarcely knew what I was doing, but I rose and drew the sheet about me like a toga. I could not wait to don my tunic. And down the steps I followed, down the street, through the gate, down the road, across the valley, always keeping a little way behind the band. Over the brook and up the side of Olivet they went, and still I followed. The great wall of the Temple courts loomed above me on the left. As we climbed the hillside I began to see the lights still burning near the altar ; and the smoke of the Paschal sacrifice going up and up till it was lost in the darkness. And then the Rabbi and His disciples halted under the great cedars. I lay and watched from a distance behind an aged bole. I saw eight of the band lie down not far from where I watched, and soon they were all asleep. I saw the other four go a little farther on into the wood. Then three of them halted and sat down,—apparently to watch. The solitary Figure went still farther on into the wood. Darkly I caught glimpses of them by the struggling light of the Paschal moon, through the hazy sky and the shadows of the great trees. One by one the three watchers sank wearily to sleep. Sometimes I fancied I caught stray sounds of a voice—lonely and sorrowful sounds, heart-rending to hear. Sometimes it seemed like pleading, sometimes like sobbing. The chill hand of fear clutched closer on my heart. And then, hark! was it the sound of a distant night-wind hurrying over the tree-tops; was it the cry of the pariah dogs echoing up the valley from Hinnom? Nearer and nearer crept the sound, and then the light of the torches flickering and bobbing. I caught the glint of armour. There were Roman soldiers there. They passed quite close. I heard their hoarse voices. I saw figures armed with staves, and I recognised some hired bravos of the Temple. Bent on evil! And leading in front—yes, it was the same stoop, the same uncertain step—the man who had left the upper room alone.

" I hardly know what followed, for in a moment all was confusion and alarm. But I rose and crept nearer. There was a short struggle, the flash of a sword in the moonlight, and then the friends of the Rabbi scattered and fled. And there He stood, alone in the midst of the mob, bound with thongs. Was it a boy's eager curiosity, or was it something deeper that drew me nearer? Some of the rabble turned to take me, but I struggled free, save that some one held my linen sheet. There was another sword-slash, and I let go and fled, naked, yelling with terror and pain.

" For days I was at home nursing my wound. And when the little company began to straggle back to my father's house, I crept into the room beside them. I carried up their food, for I was eager to listen to their talk, to find out what had happened. And there was one of them, a great, strong, rugged man, who seemed most sorrowful and remorseful of all. And I pitied him, and tried to show him kindness in my stammering, embarrassed way. And he was grateful, and asked about my wounded hand.

" I shall never forget the evening when he came in all smiles. He could not tell us clearly what had occurred. He had met the Master—risen from the grave, he said. And then a strange thing happened. The men ceased their lamentations, and began to pray. And their words were very quiet and full of joy. And the evening dusk grew very holy. Somebody else seemed to be in the room, and they talked to Him. I could not see Him, but I felt the presence. And they asked Him eager questions, until their faces shone with joy. And once more they broke the bread and passed the wine, as they told me they had done the night before He died. I was moved as never before—though I did not understand then. But afterwards I did— when Peter asked me, Would you not like to be a friend of the great Master, too ? Yes, afterward I understood.

> "When faith breaks the bread and pity pours the wine,
> There is Christ's self, the Sacrament divine."

* * * *

" I can't help telling this story, because if it had never happened, I might never have become a follower of Jesus. I tell it with all its stark ignominy and humiliation because it is my chief glory now.

" Oh, and something very like it occurred to me later in my career. I was always eager for adventure, always timid in danger. Years after, in the days of the great famine in the Holy City, when Paul and Barnabas arrived with a gift for the starving Christians, they stayed in our house, and I helped them in the distribution of the gift. I heard them talking of a great crusade they were planning—the carrying of the Gospel far afield to the Gentiles. The adventure of it drew me and I was eager to go, and when they left the city they took me with them. I was ill-prepared for the journey— just like that night when I had only my linen cloth about me. I hadn't counted the cost.

" I saw them set apart for the great adventure. I sailed with them from the port of Antioch. I passed with them through Cyprus, and with Barnabas visited our friends in the island. But the work was hard, and there were sneers and indifference to meet, insult and scorn. And by-and-by we set sail for the mainland—out into the unknown ; and I began to be afraid. Paul was ill when we landed, but I was amazed at the burning passion of the man, so eager to go on. There was no turning back with him. Then we set out on the terrible journey. I shall never forget the terror of it. Up and up we toiled, worn out, fatigued, exhausted, hungry often, into the great passes of the Taurus Mountains. There were perils of rivers in flood to encounter, perils of avalanche ; we were cold and shelterless oftentimes, and robbers haunted the way. And then one night my heart failed me, and I—I fled— home to the shelter of my mother's house. The memory of the shame of that journey will never leave me. I was stripped of all my hardihood—

naked, just like that dread night in Gethsemane, when I fled naked and terror-stricken home. Oh, the months of remorse, conscience-stricken and ashamed! And then I heard that Paul and Barnabas had returned to Antioch, and my mother counselled me to go and make a clean breast of it to them, and plead to be pardoned. And Barnabas was kind, and comforted me. "Son of Consolation" the disciples called him, and he was that to me. It was just like the Risen Christ forgiving me—as He did in the days that followed the Cross, when Peter told me the story of His dying love.

"And Paul was gentle, too, but he would not trust me again. And Barnabas would not go without me—he was like the Master, who said He would never leave nor forsake His weak, wavering followers. So Paul separated from us, and Barnabas and I went to Cyprus again. I was eager to retrieve my character, eager to win back the trust of the great Paul. We had many hardships, many hours of disappointment and despondency in Cyprus. But I fought and fought with my fears. And then our fellow-countrymen grew enraged at us when we began to win disciples for the Lord. And Barnabas was arrested and I saw him die. I was in terror and would have fled again. But a wonderful thing happened. When I saw my dear friend die, it seemed to me that I was witnessing what had happened in Jerusalem—Calvary's Cross all over again, and I caught one overpowering sight of the love of God. A great peace entered my heart and I was no longer afraid. I, too, was ready to die for Christ who had died for me. Nay, it was Christ who had come to me and entered my heart. From that day on, He has been my companion and friend.

" Paul heard of me and wanted to see me, and I travelled to Rome. And when I saw the prisoner in chains I wept, and he fell on my neck and kissed me. Then Peter came to Rome—he who had first won me for the Master, and I joined myself to him. O, the wonder of those days, toiling for the Master far from home, yet never for one moment alone. Often, as I went about the world with Peter, and saw the great change come over poor and insignificant men—slaves, outcasts—and saw them holding true to Christ through jeering, abuse, torture, pain and death, He came to me and spoke to me ; and still He comes to me and speaks to me, and I know He is alive."

CHAPTER III

Another Story of the House of the Upper Room

SOME thirty odd years after the night of the Last Supper in the Upper Room at Jerusalem, a vessel set sail from Cæsarea, bearing passengers on board who were bound for Rome. It was to all appearances the last stage of one of the most momentous careers in the world's history. The central figure was a prisoner, under escort of Roman soldiers. Two friends had made up their minds to accompany him ; and as he was a first-class prisoner, they were allowed to register themselves as attendants. One of them kept a journal, and on the second or third day of the voyage, as the journal informs us, " We had to sail under the lee of Cyprus, for the wind was against us." One feels sure that the three men —who were none other than Paul and Aristarchus of Thessalonica and the doctor, Luke, who tells the story from his diary—were on deck as the ship rounded the eastmost point of the island ; and that Paul spent a long time gazing wistfully towards the mainland, where the city of his youth and boyhood, Tarsus, lay. For he himself felt, as his address to the elders of Ephesus a few months previously makes manifest, that it was his last long look at his native land. But he must have turned also now and then, as past memories came crowding in upon him, to look at the island of Cyprus—affection, self-reproach, and sadness meeting in his eyes. And to ease his aching heart he must have told again a chapter of the story of his past.

We believe that this story is to be found, almost as it was told, in the book of Acts (xi. 19-xiii. 13). It is just at the close of this story that Luke, as an eye-witness of the great events which followed, takes up the tale. And note the order of the incidents in this narrative which we think came mainly from the lips of Paul. The first word is a reference to the martyrdom of Stephen. That it was as the result of this tragedy that the great mission to the Gentiles first began, was something that Paul, who was consenting to Stephen's death, could never forget. His own life as the chief propagandist of that Gentile mission was a noble atonement for his false step ; that mistake accounts in part for the life-long zeal with which he pursued his task. And it is the scattering of the Christians from Jerusalem in the terror that followed the murder of Stephen, with the consequent first proclaiming of the Gospel to the Greeks in Antioch, that is next recorded in the narrative here. Then —for this was the main burden of Paul's story to his friends—comes the mention of Barnabas. A noble description it is—" a good man, full of the Holy Spirit and of faith." It reads like an echo from the stricken heart of Paul, to whom the memory of an old quarrel was speaking its sad reproach. Next, as we might expect, comes the story of how Barnabas found him out after his eleven years' seclusion in Tarsus, and rescued him for Christ's work. Then follows the account of the first important bit of Christian work they did together—the bearing of the famine relief-fund to Jerusalem.

Another Story of the Upper Room

And then—apparently a long interruption. It is really no interruption at all. The visit to Jerusalem recalls the house where they stayed, and the house recalls a remarkable incident which happened there a year or two before. And the son of the house is mentioned—inevitably—for it is over him that the two friends quarrelled and separated; and that is the burden of Paul's confession to his friends. For note how the digression ends : " and Barnabas and Saul returned from Jerusalem when they had fulfilled their ministry, and took with them John, whose surname was Mark."

These, then, were the memories that moved Paul as he stood on the deck of the ship that day, while they sailed under the lee of Cyprus. And it is some hidden links of the story that we wish now to tell. It is a very instructive fact that while Christianity began as a working-class movement, many of the men who played a great part in its propagation were what we might call university men—Joseph of Arimathæa, Paul, Luke, Apollos. It is with yet another that we are now concerned.

I

Tarsus, the city in whose streets Paul played as a boy, was a flourishing town, as renowned for its culture as its commerce. According to Strabo, at its hey-day its zeal for learning surpassed even that of Athens and Alexandria. And the view of life which was chiefly taught within the gates of its University was Stoicism. The founder of Stoicism, Zeno, was born in Cyprus ; Cleanthes, the second great teacher of this view of life, was a native of Assos, in the Troad ; and Chrysippus, the third leader of the movement, hailed from Soli, which was actually in the province of Cilicia. The very atmosphere of Asia Minor seems to have been peculiarly favourable to the growth of such thinking. Epictetus was born in Hierapolis in Phrygia.

The Stoic teachers in Tarsus were generally natives of the place. Antipater flourished there a generation or two before Paul's day ; and Atheno-dorus may have been an older contemporary. Students came from all parts; and any youth of Cyprus who had an ambition to be a scholar, would naturally cross over to the mainland to attend the lectures of the professors at the University of Tarsus.

About the time that Christ was born, there was a Jewish family, the household of Nebo, which had settled in Cyprus, acquired property in the rich garden lands of the island, and grown wealthy in consequence. One of the sons of this man was a lad named Joseph, a tall lad with a grave and noble face : he was destined one day to be regarded as a god by a city mob—even as the supreme god in the Pantheon. His father's family seems to have belonged to the tribe of Levi in older days. And very probably the father had ambitions that his son should be educated, and eventually go to Jerusalem, and take his place as one of the Levites, the lesser priests of the great Temple. The boy himself had yearnings after knowledge. So by-and-by he was sent to Tarsus to be educated, for not all Jews, even among the stricter sort, despised the pagan culture.

Now there was a Jewish tent-maker in Tarsus who kept very strictly to the ancient faith. He had a sickly son, " small in stature, . . . bandy-legged, but well built, with meeting eye-brows, and slightly prominent nose " (*Acts of Paul and*

Thecla).   But he was a lad " full of grace," for he
" sometimes had the aspect of an angel " (*Ibid.*).
He was somewhat younger than Joseph.   Whether
they met at the University we cannot tell.   But it
seems very likely that they met in Tarsus in these
early days.   For the loyal-hearted Joseph was the
only friend Saul had in Jerusalem once—commending
him to his former enemies when he was under a
cloud.   Joseph might possibly have lodged at the
tent-maker's house.   For a Jew would naturally
look out for a lodging in a Jewish home.   They
would worship together in the Jewish synagogue
of the place, at any rate.   And the sickly Saul's
strict Pharisaic father would be one of the leading men
of that congregation.   The early acquaintanceship
between these two—the small, pale lad with the
burning, eager spirit, and the tall, strong youth with
the grave and noble face—was perhaps one of the
stories which Saul, now called Paul, would tell his
companions, Luke and Aristarchus, as they sailed
between Cyprus and the mainland on that
memorable voyage to Rome.

The strictness of Paul's upbringing may have
precluded him from attending the University.
But, if he did not, it is certain that he imbibed the
intellectual ideas, and breathed to some purpose the
spiritual atmosphere of the place.   There is evidence
that the noble if somewhat arid way of thinking of
the Stoics quickened his mental agility, broadened
his outlook, and gave him several suggestive
points of view which were just needing to be
baptised into Christ to become living and fruitful.
The real truth that lurks in Stoic Pantheism never
found juster expression, never was put to nobler
service, than when Paul told the Athenians, " The

LORD of heaven and earth dwelleth not in temples made with hands, neither is He worshipped with men's hands as though He needed anything, seeing He giveth to all life and breath and all things, and hath made of one blood all nations of men . . . that they should seek the LORD, if haply they might feel after Him and find Him, though He be not far from every one of us. For in Him we live and move and have our being ; as certain also of your own poets have said, ' For we are also His offspring ' " (Acts xvii. 28). Or when he wrote to the Corinthians: "There is one God, the Father, from whom all comes, and for whom we exist." Or to the Romans : " All comes from Him, all lives by Him, all ends in Him." Or to the Ephesians " There is . . . One God and Father of all who is over us all, who pervades us all, who is within us all."

Nor was there ever a more daring adaptation of the Stoic " logos "-doctrine than when Paul said of Jesus : " He is the image of the invisible God, the first-born of every creature ; for by Him were all things created . . . and for Him ; He is before all things, and in Him all things cohere." Again the Stoic doctrine of the spiritual unity of mankind is surely reflected in the pregnant figure of the Body and its members ; and its practical consequences announced in the effective and far-reaching principle of the fellow-citizenship of Jew and Gentile, male and female, bond and free in the Kingdom of God— the unity of all, the new creation of all, and the consequent equality of all, in Christ (cf. 1 Cor. xii. 12f, 27 ; Gal. iii. 28 ; Eph. ii. 19 ; Col. iii. 11).

In Paul's teaching, the Stoic doctrine of self-sufficiency (ἀντάρκεια) is not only reproduced but touched to a finer morality. The proud humility and meekness of his personal claim, " poor, yet making many rich, having nothing, yet possessed of all things " (2 Cor. vi. 10) ; the confidence of his exhortation : " God is able to make all grace abound towards you, that ye, always having all *sufficiency* in all things, may abound in every good work . . . being enriched in everything to all bountifulness " (2 Cor. ix. 8, 11) ; the beauty of his contented closing days : " I have learned in whatever state I am to be content (αὐτάρκης) . . . I am all-strong in Him who puts power into me. . . . I have enough and more than enough " (Phil. iv. 11, 13, 18), are very striking transformations of the Stoic teaching. He found " religion with self-sufficiency a vastly repaying thing " in life (1 Tim. vi. 6). He was familiar also with the Stoic term for " conscience " (συνείδησις)—uses it frequently ; and his interpretation of it as the divine law written on the heart of man is surely a reflection of Stoic thought (Rom. ii. 15).

Moreover we have evidence that Paul did not ban from his mind the Hellenic literary culture of the day. He can quote to good purpose the Greek poets in vogue at the time. There is a line in the first letter to Corinth which Paul had probably read in Menander, though Menander is said to have borrowed the line from Euripides :

Φθείρουσιν ἤθη χρῆσθ' ὁμιλίαι κακαί

Evil companionships corrupt good character.

Indeed, in that address of his on the Areopagus in Athens, Luke reports him as twice quoting the poets. It is the poet Aratos, who himself had studied in Tarsus, who said of the Divine Being :

τοῦ γὰρ καὶ γένος 'εσμέν

For we also are His offspring.

And when Paul says " In Him we live and move and have our being," he is quoting a sentiment of the Cretan poet-prophet, Epimenides. It was the memory of this Divine Man (Θεῖος ἀνήρ), as Plato calls him, that the sight of those altars " to an unknown god " awakened in St. Paul. It was he at whose suggestion the chastened Athenians, who had sent for him after a plague in the city, erected these anonymous altars in 596 B.C. It was he who defended the Divine Being as ever young and strong and beautiful, against the conception of Him as a dying god in the Myth of Dionysos, or reflected in the Cretan grave—so-called—of Zeus :

> The Cretans carved a tomb for thee, O holy and high !
> *Liars, evil beasts, idle gormandizers !*
> For thou dost not die, thou art ever alive and steadfast :
> Yea, *in thee we live and move and have our being.*

The second line is the line which is quoted in the letter to Titus. The passage seems to have deeply impressed itself on the mind of Paul. It was these prophetic voices in the literature of Greece that had moved him most profoundly.

The presence of these things in the writings of Paul ought to convince us that the Hellenist Jews were not despisers of the Greek culture. And, whether Paul had attended lectures in the University of Tarsus or no, it is clear evidence to us that his alert mind had drunk deep of the spirit of his age. Many a day when the young student Joseph came home from the lectures, he would be assailed by the eager questions of the younger Saul. And together they would talk gravely and earnestly about the meaning of life, this strange mystery the beginning and the end of which were lost in the mists of birth and death. What did the philosophers at the University say about it ?

Human souls, they said, came to life upon the earth out of the bosom of the great Soul that animated the whole world. For the world was not a dead thing : it was alive ; it had a mind that could think and reason. Anyone who looked long at the life of the world with earnest eyes could see that, they said. There was reason, intelligence in the plan on which the world was built. And for human souls, who in their power to think showed kinship with the Divine, the true life to live was not the life of the passions and the senses, but life according to reason, life according to Nature—a life of patience, self-sufficiency, calmness, serenity. Human souls when they died would be absorbed into the great Soul of the world again ; for this Divine life was the only life that went on for ever and ever. Thus the only true life to live was a life attuned to that of the great Soul of Nature. . . .

So these two lads talked about Eternal life. But it was sad and grey and gloomy teaching for young souls panting for more life and fuller. By way of contrast to it, the only system of thought that seemed to have religious attraction at the time was the Pythagorean. It was a reaction against the pantheistic conception, which meant the ultimate extinction of the soul. For Pythagoreanism maintained a doctrine of the transmigration of souls— a doctrine which said that souls at death were reincarnated in other bodies—the bodies of animals —to work out the evil entail of their previous life upon the earth. Often has the crux of philosophical contendings turned about this age-long problem of the soul's destiny. The young men weighed the contending views. The problem had become acute. It had for the most part slumbered unanswered in the bosom of their own Faith, and now that the question was awake, this ancient Faith, save for a few isolated cries, had nothing to offer that could give them lasting peace.

II

It came about that when Joseph had completed his studies at Tarsus, he was sent up to Jerusalem to be trained for Levitical service. This wealthy family of Cyprus had relatives in Jerusalem. Joseph bar-Nebo had an aunt, a sister of his father, who was married to a Jerusalemite. It was to the house of his father's sister that this rich young man would be sent to stay. Who was this lady?

It is here that the meaning of the digression in the story Paul told to his companions that day as they sailed under the lee of Cyprus becomes plain. It was to tell of the beginning of his acquaintanceship with the man who had been the cause of the rupture between himself and his friend. No doubt he was easing his heavy heart by accepting his share of the blame, nay, perhaps taking it all to himself. " It was sad and foolish," Paul was fain to confess, " and I was hasty ; but it is all over now. Joseph bar-Nebo was too big-hearted a man to harbour a grudge, and we became good friends again " (*cf.* 1 Cor. ix. 6). " From what I hear John Mark and he may be labouring at this hour in Cyprus. Perhaps I was too severe on Mark. By his labours he has re-instated himself in my good opinion. I wish I could see him again."

Paul's wish was by-and-by fulfilled. And in the sentence from his letters which makes this clear, we learn at last the exact connection between Joseph Bar-Nebo and the house of the Upper Room. "Aristarchus, my fellow-prisoner saluteth you," he writes to the Church in Colossæ, "and Marcus, sister's son to Barnabas." Mark was Joseph's cousin. And the house where Joseph the student from Cyprus stayed when he was training for the office of Levite in the Holy City was the house of the Upper Room! The lady of the house, Joseph's aunt, is John Mark's mother. What memories begin to cluster about that house in Jerusalem!

III

The hidden and romantic side of the story is still to come. It is an extraordinarily attractive story, and if nothing more than a great deal of likelihood can be claimed for it, it is nevertheless worth the telling.

After Joseph Bar-Nebo's training was over, he in due course became a Levite (Acts iv. 36). This is the only time that a Levite is mentioned by name in the New Testament, and perhaps we shall find that Luke has a reason for so designating Joseph here. The Levites served at the altar in courses, and Joseph's fortnight would come round twice a year. Naturally the young man would no longer stay with his aunt, but would set up house for himself elsewhere. Now the place where a great many of the priests stayed during the eleven months when they were not on duty at the Temple, was not in Jerusalem but down in the pleasant garden city of Jericho, in the Jordan valley. They were always passing up and down the road from Jerusalem to Jericho. It gives us a very vivid insight into the skill of Jesus as a story-teller to observe that when He told of the man who was waylaid by thieves on that road, He pictures the two who passed by on the other side as a priest and a Levite. Of course whenever Joseph came up to Jerusalem he would always pay a visit to his relatives in the house of the Upper Room. He was a big, strong, great-hearted, friendly soul; no doubt his very much younger cousin John Mark adored him. He was the boy's hero; they were great friends.

We must build the next part of the story for ourselves. One day Joseph, when he called, found that something great and wonderful had happened in the home. His father's sister and her husband were transformed. They had always been serious-minded folk, but now they seemed full of some unutterable happiness. They could not tell their priestly nephew what it was, but neither could they hide it; and the sight must have awakened the old yearnings in his heart—the yearning and questioning about life, that had troubled him in far-off Tarsus: how to win true life, life abiding and eternal, how to reach satisfaction. For this was what his uncle and aunt seemed to be—satisfied. And yet they were comparatively unimportant people. As for him, he had reached the height of his own and his father's ambition. He was a rich man; he owned land; he had all that this life could give him in the way of ease and comfort. He was a minister of their holy religion in the Temple. But still he was not satisfied. He had often felt the hollowness and sham of all this gorgeous ceremony. And his associates, the priests, the Sadducees—so many of them were just greedy, grasping worldlings. They were anything but religious. They laughed mockingly at the thought of the life to come; they believed it was all moonshine. Yes, something was lacking in his life—what was it? Perhaps the boy, John Mark, had let fall some innocent talk, about a gracious Stranger that had visited their home, and become the friend of his parents. Joseph had heard rumours of the Prophet of Galilee, extraordinary rumours they were. And he wondered if this could be He. And so down in his fine villa in Jericho, surrounded with luxury, he was restless, ill at ease. The old yearning had broken out again. . . .

At length the Prophet of Galilee appeared in Jericho. It was on His return journey from the Feast of Booths, whither He had gone, not in a public capacity, but as a private pilgrim (*cf.* John vii. 10, x. 40). Returning to His headquarters in the Peræa, He must needs pass through Jericho. The inmates of the house of the Upper Room may have been friends of Jesus earlier than this, but certainly they must have known Him by the time of this Feast. For it was all but His last visit to the Holy City before the Passion, and they were familiar friends of His by then. Almost certainly He must have heard from these friends about the wealthy and noble young Levite with the unsatisfied heart, who sometimes talked with sighs about his old student days in Tarsus, and his Stoic philosophy of life, life according to Nature, life full and abiding, the life for which he longed and longed. Certain it is that Jesus went into a synagogue at Jericho, and rose to speak, on the ruler's invitation to the stranger. What was it that Jesus talked about that day? Have we no hint? A certain captious lawyer stood up at the close of His address, and asked, " What shall I do to inherit *eternal life* ? "

Does it not seem as if Jesus had deliberately chosen that as the theme of His address—Life, True Life, Life abiding and eternal ? And it was in answer to the lawyer that He told the story of the Good Samaritan. Was it a mere chance thrust—that reference to the Levite who came and looked at the wounded man, and then—passed by ? Perhaps the ruler of the Synagogue could tell !

Some months after, and somewhere in the neighbourhood of Jericho, as Jesus was coming out of a house on to the highway, a man of great possessions, who had evidently been on the outlook for Jesus, saw Him and ran after Him, and kneeling at His feet asked earnestly, anxiously, breathlessly, " Good Master, what must I do to inherit *eternal life ?* " " *Good* Master ? " Jesus answered. " Why do you call me good ? Have you ever learned the true meaning of goodness ? You have lived a moral life, you have possibly escaped the temptations that beset a young man's way. Perhaps you are beginning to think that goodness is just a human achievement, and easy. My son, God alone is good. All goodness comes from Him. Have you never found that out ?—Have you kept all the commandments ? And the man answered, wearily, disappointedly, " All these have I kept from my youth up. But I am not satisfied ; what lack I yet ? " And Jesus, when He looked into his noble, open, manly face, and saw the deep, deep questioning in his eyes, loved him. Yet the swift and terrible thrust followed : " Go, sell all that you have, and give to the poor. And come, follow me." And when the man heard it he went away sorrowful, for he had great possessions.

Why is this disappointing story told in the

Another Story of the Upper Room

Gospels—the story, seemingly, of Jesus' failure, His unsuccess ? *Was* He in the long run unsuccessful with this suppliant ? We cannot believe it. Unsatisfied, unhappy, in such deep, tragic earnestness about the highest things—and such a beautiful soul, for Jesus loved him at first sight ; no, no, it cannot be the completed story. Look closer at the narrative and see. It has long been the fashion to pause at the words " he went away sorrowful," as if that were the Gospel ending of the tale. But that is to miss the whole point of Mark's narrative. The true end of the story is Jesus' confident word, " With God *all* things are possible." John Mark would never have told it, if that were the end—that sorrowful departure. For though the other Gospels add some details, Mark's is the most moving story, and it forms the basis for the others' version. Not only has it this note of unwavering hopefulness at the end, but it is Mark alone who remembers the touching fact that Jesus loved him. And it is Mark who maintains the deepest reticence about the man. It looks as though he could have told the end of the story, if only it had come within the scope of his narrative about the earthly ministry of Jesus.

And what is the meaning of this reticence in the Gospels ? None of them tell the man's name. The evangelists frequently manifest this delicacy of feeling. There is a Christian reserve of temper in the telling of the story of Judas, as if there were friends in the early circle of Christians whom unrestrained censure would have pained. There is a delicacy of reference to the case of the Magdalene, as if there were some prominent and loved member of the early Church whom it deeply concerned. But that is another story. The same reserve is apparent here. Is it the story of a prominent Christian among the early followers of the Nazarene ? He was known in the early Church, though Mark merely calls him " one " ($\epsilon\hat{\imath}s$—an Aramaism which reveals that it was so he had been named in the first telling of the story). For in Matthew, the Palestinian Gospel, the Gospel of the Jerusalem Church, it is noted that he was young (Matt xix. 20, 22), and Luke knew all about him, too, for he alone tells us that he was a ruler ($\check{\alpha}\rho\chi\omega\nu$), *i.e.*, a synagogue ruler, in all probability.

Is the reason for John Mark's reticence that the man was his own cousin Joseph ? If Jesus loved him as He gazed on the noble form, might he not well be the man whom the citizens of Lystra mistook for a god in the likeness of men ? We should expect the cousin of Mark to be a young man at the time of this incident. And who more likely to be a ruler of a synagogue in Jericho than a Levite, a man of wealth and lands, who had made Jericho his home ?

It was a man of great possessions, himself seeking to fulfil the divine stewardship, who first suggested this solution of the story to the writer. " Do you not think," he said, " that this rich young ruler came at last to Christ in the days that followed Calvary ? " And together we turned to the book of Acts (iv. 32), and read these words :

" Now there was but one heart and soul among all those who had embraced the faith ; none of them claimed any of his possessions as his own, they shared all they had with one another. And in fact there was not a needy man among them, for all who were possessors of lands or houses sold them, and brought the money which they realised, laying it before the feet of the Apostles ; it was then distributed according to each one's need. Thus Joseph, who was surnamed Barnabas, or (as it may be translated) ' Son of Encouragement,' by the Apostles, a Levite of Cypriote birth, *sold an estate which he had, and brought the money, which he placed before the feet of the Apostles."*

The first rich man to sell his possessions and give to the poor when he gave his whole heart to Jesus ! Doubtless it was in the Upper Room this incident occurred—the place where Jesus had manifested Himself to His disciples after Calvary. It was the nearest possible to a literal fulfilling of the command, " Sell all that you have and give to the poor, and come, follow me "—the nearest possible with the Cross between. As we watch the dramatic and sacramental action, do we not feel constrained to say, This is the rich young ruler at last ? We can almost hear his confession to the Apostles :

" I have resolved to become a follower of your Master, Christ. Weeks ago I sought Him out, and asked the way to eternal life. But His command seemed too hard for me, too high. ' It is too difficult,' I said in self-justification. ' It would spoil and wrong the poor.' In truth, I—I was reluctant to part with my all. But He has made it easy for me. What is my poor wealth beside the wealth He poured to the death for us men, for me ? What possessions of mind, what riches of heart, what power of will, what purity, what love ! A king's ransom—a God's ransom, it was! And I come because He calls—I have felt His call again. Here in this place, where He came back to you after death, where His blessed presence was felt, was seen, I come to lay my possessions at your feet— at His feet. He knows the rest. Henceforward

I am His—I give myself to His cause; always and only now, all that I have, all that I am, is His."

"Son of Encouragement," the Apostles called him. It is a happy pun upon his ancestral name: bar-Nebo becomes bar-Nabas indeed. What would be more heartening to the disciples than to have had this great acquisition in the early days—at Pentecost? The Lord Jesus completing an unfinished story! And not merely a man of possessions, but a Temple Levite: what would Jesus not yet accomplish? And when Luke reminds us that he was a Levite, may he not be referring back significantly to that word inserted in his Gospel alone— "a ruler"? And the man proved a tower of strength to the early Church. He had the prophetic gift—"full of the Holy Spirit and of faith"—able to exercise the function of comfort, exhortation. Everybody trusted him. Large-hearted, courageously reaching the hand of fellowship to his old friend Saul, the converted persecutor—saving him from ostracism, saving him for the Gospel ministry. And when Saul, disheartened by his reception in Jerusalem, slipped away home to Tarsus, and spent eleven years there, doubtless witnessing to the new faith, but lost apparently to the Church, it was Barnabas, labouring among the Gentiles in Antioch, who remembered him and went off with unwearied hope to Tarsus; found him, and brought him to Antioch—to become the great Apostle of the Gentiles by-and-by. Fail? Nay, Jesus had not despaired of Barnabas when he turned away sorrowful, but found him out—after the Cross—at Pentecost. Jesus did not fail. Jesus had reserved a great rôle for the rich young man to play in the founding and spreading of His Kingdom in the world. Yes, truly with *God* all things are possible!

> I pleaded outlaw-wise,
> By many a hearted casement, curtained red,
>   Trellised with intertwining charities;
> (For though I knew His love who followèd,
>   Yet was I sore adread
> Lest, having Him, I must have naught beside).
>   But, if one little casement parted wide,
>   The gust of His approach would clash it to.
>   Fear wist not to evade as Love wist to pursue. . . .
>   Nigh and nigh draws the chase,
>   With unperturbèd pace,
>   Deliberate speed, majestic instancy,
>   And past those noisèd feet
>   A voice comes yet more fleet—
> "Lo! naught contents Thee, who content'st not Me!"

*　　　*　　　*　　　*

An afterword to the story may be permitted, ere the chapter closes. For the marks of probability are not yet exhausted. There is another fact which brings the likelihood close to the verge of certainty. Barnabas was known in the early Church as an *Apostle*. Now, besides the Twelve, there are only four, at the very utmost six, men to whom that title is ever applied in the New Testament. What was it that gave one the right to the name in the eyes of the first Christians? A definite and direct call of God felt and recognised by the Church as such was no doubt necessary. And Barnabas did receive such a sacramentally recognised call (Acts xiii. 3). But there are others equally graced by the Spirit who are not called Apostles in the New Testament. No doubt also they had to be men whose works showed the visible signs and fruits of Apostleship. Paul appeals to that when he makes his own claim (2 Cor. xii. 12). But many powerful evangelists, who did great work, as recorded in the New Testament, were nevertheless not called Apostles.

There was one definite and decisive test of apostleship which strictly limited the possession of the title to a few. When the disciples proceeded to elect one to fill the vacant place of Judas, they laid down this condition : the candidates must be chosen from " the men who have been associated with us all the time that the Lord Jesus went in and out among us, from the Baptism of John down to the day when He was taken up from us . . . a witness to His resurrection." These were the qualifications which Matthias, and no doubt also his fellow-nominee, Joseph Bar-sabbas (surnamed Justus) possessed. Briefly, they must have seen Jesus and received His risen Spirit. It may not be possible to say with certainty that Andronicus and Junias, whom Paul calls his " fellow-countrymen and fellow-prisoners, men of note among the Apostles, who have been in Christ longer than I," were actually Apostles ; though, since they were in Christ before him, they were probably in the company of the Upper Room on whom the Holy Spirit fell, and may have been first followers of Jesus (Rom. xvi. 7).

It is possible, though doubtful, that Silas had received the designation (1 Thess. ii. 6), but it is very likely that he had been one of the Seventy, and so would also answer to this test. It is these qualifications no doubt which entitled James, the brother of the Lord, to be called an Apostle later. But besides these just mentioned there are only two others named "Apostles" in the New Testament—Paul and Barnabas. Does Paul answer to this test ?   Let him speak for himself ?   " Am not I an apostle ? " he writes to the Corinthians, " . . . have not I seen Jesus Christ our Lord ? " (1 Cor. ix. 1.).   It may have been that he saw Christ in the flesh (2 Cor. v. 16), but in any case his vivid vision of the risen Christ on the road to Damascus is here claimed by him as a sufficient fulfilment of the test (*cf.* 1 Cor. xv. 8).   Barnabas seems to have been finally won for Christ at Pentecost, but though he may have shared the Pentecostal experience which was a demonstration of the resurrection, there was no actual vision of Christ at that time. Thus, if we are to claim for him a complete fulfilment of the test, we must postulate some actual contact with Jesus in the days of His flesh.   May not the story we have told here plead to be recognised as the circumstance which makes good that claim ?

CHAPTER IV

The First Witness for Christian Liberty

IT is too often the fate of great words to become merely the objects of admiring contemplation. Spoken by a great soul, they lie dormant in the mind of the race—until the arrival of another great soul in whose heart they start into life and pass out into action.

The story of the first Christian martyrdom is a familiar story. Christianity has enshrined the name of Stephen as the first on the roll that is written in letters of blood and fire. And it may be objected that there is nothing obscure in the record of Stephen to justify our making it one of the hidden romances of the New Testament. But it is only a single chapter in the life of Stephen—the last—and only the external aspect of it—the tragedy of the end—on which the thoughts of the Church have been mainly concentrated. We have been too much engrossed in the spectacular side of the short career ; too little concerned with the great deed of liberation which was the cause of that end. We have read his defence on the day of his trial too often as an interesting but somewhat irrelevant piece of national history which was abruptly terminated before we could see the point he was making. Its piercing and poignant *relevance* is too often missed.

It was more a deed than a speech—an act in which Christianity was rent violently from the position of a mere sectarian out-growth on the parent tree of Judaism ; a rending which decided the fate of Judaism as the religion of Law, and of Christianity as the religion of the Spirit.

It was Jesus who reminded men of the evil fate of sewing new cloth on old, of putting new wine in old wineskins. Matthew recorded the words admiringly in his diary ; but Matthew himself, we are told, became a legalist. It was reserved for Stephen to rend the new and the old apart—to burst the antique wineskin. Judaism could not be leavened for Christ. It could only be revolutionised —shattered and remoulded. And the Christian community was at first divided. One party clung to the hope of leavening. They regarded the new Faith as only an addition and completion of the old. They regarded themselves as a new party *within* the ancient Faith. They clung to the Temple worship. They went up daily to prayers (Acts iii. 1). But it was the corrupt leaven of the ancient Faith that leavened *them*. They by-and-by faded away into a legalistic sect ; they passed out of the stream of religious life, and became stagnant pools of the desert—Judaisers, Ebionites, Nazarenes, Elkesaites. The living stream of Christian faith flowed into other channels. And it was through the broken body of Stephen that the passage was cleft for the water which flowed from the cleft Rock, Christ crucified.

Who was the man ? And what was the disturbing truth he taught, which led the Jews to do him to death ? How did his influence live on in the subsequent history of Christianity ?

He was the most distinguished member of the first Ecclesiastical Committee that was ever elected by the Christian Church—probably its convener. And this Committee was chosen because Christianity was spreading so fast in Jerusalem that the Twelve Apostles, who were natives of Palestine, and whose language was the Hebrew dialect known as Aramaic, were finding it impossible to look after the interests of the many Greek-speaking Jews—Jews of the Dispersion—who had been won for the new faith in Jerusalem. This young man with the Greek name was the most outstanding of the Hellenist Jews who had accepted Christ in the early days. He was obviously not a native of Palestine. He belonged originally to one of the many Jewish colonies or settlements which were scattered here and there all round the shores of the Mediterranean in the chief commercial centres of the Roman Empire.

Very obviously, too, he was possessed of the gift of eloquence ; and when he became a Christian he soon stood out as one of the most arresting and powerful of all the first pleaders for Christ.

Jerusalem was not only the city of the Holy Temple ; there were numerous synagogues dotted all over the town. And when these Jewish colonists returned to the city either for temporary or for permanent residence there, they clubbed together and worshipped in a synagogue of their own. In this story we read of " the synagogue which is called the synagogue of the Libyans (for so most probably the word should be rendered), the Cyrenians, and the Alexandrians ; as well as that of the Cilicians and Asiatics." Correctly interpreted, this verse refers to *two* synagogues, not five. One was the synagogue in which the Jewish colonists of the South forgathered. To it resorted the African Jews.

who are named here " in the geographical order of their original dwelling-places." The other was the synagogue in which the Jews of the North met— Jews from Asia Minor, or, as they are named here, Jews from the provinces of Cilicia and Asia. This interpretation makes the verse not only intelligible, but full of significance for the story we are now considering. There was a young man who had come down all the way from the city of Tarsus in Cilicia to be a student in the House of the Midrash, the sacred college of the Jews. Naturally this student, far from home, would attend the services in the synagogue where he would be likely to meet acquaintances from his native town, or at any rate people from that quarter. The young man's name was Saul.

Where did Stephen hail from ? We are not told in so many words, but certain details of the narrative all point in the one direction. In the verse we have just quoted (Acts vi. 9), it is the synagogue of the Southern colonials which is mentioned first. They seem to have been the chief movers against the young heretic. It was they whom he had troubled most by the persistent advocacy of his new views. The connection of Philip the Evangelist with this tragic incident is also suggestive. Luke indeed may have got certain details of the story from him. Philip was the next most distinguished member of the committee of Seven elected to look after the interests of the colonial Jews who had become Christians in Jerusalem. He was evidently a close friend of Stephen. There is a tradition that the two went out together to evangelise among the Samaritans. And after Stephen's death Philip fled from Jerusalem. A close friend of Stephen would be a marked man in the city. It is noteworthy that his flight, after a brief and troubled sojourn in Samaria, was in the direction of the South. We observe, too, his interest in the Ethiopian State-Treasurer who passed him in his chariot reading a remarkable book which he had apparently picked up on a stall in the city while there on a pilgrimage of faith. Philip's eagerness to get a friendly lift from this pilgrim from the land of Egypt reveals the direction in which his thoughts were turning. And for a time thereafter Philip's whereabouts were unknown (*cf.* Acts viii. 39f.). Had he gone to Stephen's home to carry the sad news to his friends ?

Most moving and suggestive of all is the fact that Saul of Tarsus, who was a party to the murder of Stephen, *never* in all his amazing missionary enterprises—never once—turned his eyes towards the Southern seaboards of the Mediterranean. Was it that he felt he could not possibly be received with favour in quarters that still rang with the horror of their countryman Stephen's death ? Never once did he turn his eyes toward Alexandria where there were many thousands of Jews, with a university of their own, which was fast rising into fame and spreading the influence of its culture all over the East. Never once did he think of visiting this city of that eloquent fellow-worker of his—Apollos. It is no rash conjecture that Stephen was a Southerner, and that very likely his early home was Alexandria.

Nor can we help feeling strongly that he had come to Jerusalem for the same reason as Saul of Tarsus. He had perhaps studied philosophy in the Jewish College of Alexandria. He was another of the many souls, in that time of universal religious yearning, who wanted to probe deeper. Perhaps he had hopes that he himself might become a teacher of religion in some synagogue of the Dispersion ; and had come up to Jerusalem to finish his training in the Law at the Divinity College there, in the precincts of the Temple. These two young men were strangers ; they attended different places of worship on the Sabbath, for Stephen would attend the African synagogue. The conjecture which has been made—that they may actually have sat on the same bench at college, listening to the lectures of the great Gamaliel—is quite a possible one. It could hardly have been later than Pentecost of 29 A.D. that Stephen was won for Christ. And though the dates are uncertain, Saul may have been a student in Jerusalem about the time of the Crucifixion. Saul was still a young man at the time of Stephen's death (Acts vii. 58), though he seems already to have risen to ecclesiastical prominence— acting as a kind of sheriff-officer of the Sanhedrin (Acts viii. 3, ix. 1), if not indeed as a voting member (Acts xxvi. 10). Stephen and he were both in Jerusalem together at the most impressionable period of their lives. And students from a distance were almost certain to attend the most famous of the Jewish professors or Rabbis.

They would present a striking contrast as they sat there side by side. The Tarsian, a diminutive youth, nervous and awkward in manner, his talk broken and rapid, his possibly light-coloured hair already thinning, cheeks gaunt and pale, high ascetic brow, and red-lidded eyes sore and weak, though in the dark heart of them there burned a fierce fire. A Pharisee of the Pharisees in his upbringing and outlook, rigid, intolerant, scornful, proud. The other a handsome youth with noble, open, manly face, olive-complexioned—the red blood glowing in his cheeks from the fiery kisses of the Southern sun. Perhaps he had the dark, straight hair that bespoke the Jew, but we like to think of him as differing from the rule of his race in possessing eyes the colour of heaven's blue ; he had a Greek name and probably his father or mother was Greek.

The philosophy of Alexandria was mystical in its tendency, and the comtemplative faculty had been awakened in his soul. He was a dreamer, and his dreams wandered far beyond the bounds of the Jewish Law. Did not his teachers in Alexandria study the Greek culture, and try to interpret their ancient faith in terms of its philosophy ? If ever he had talked with Saul of Tarsus, he would find that their outlook on things was whole worlds apart,— Stephen dreaming of a universal religion, ready to admit that anywhere men could find communion with God ; Saul contemptuous of every faith but his own, and believing that the Holy Temple alone was the place where men might find perfect communion with God.

Had they ever seen Jesus in the flesh ? There is nothing in Paul's writings that really contradicts the assertion. When he says " we have known Christ after the flesh," there may be at least the suggestion of contact with the historic Personality. For he afterwards had a vision of Christ, and recognition of the Figure seems to imply an actual sight of Jesus at some earlier time. It does not debar us from thinking that he was in Jerusalem that solemn Passover week, to be reminded that he never refers to it in his writings. He knew many things about Christ which he never mentions in his letters.

He must have taught many things about Him which he does not repeat with the pen. His writings are to confirm his readers in the great *truths* of the Gospel, not to give the facts of the story. And once at least in that stormy and excited Pascha week the great Figure may have passed before his eyes, the iconoclast Reformer who was gibbeted on a Cross. It is round that Cross that all Paul's doctrine gathers.

Somehow one feels surer about the case of Stephen. In an ecstasy of waking vision he, too, saw Jesus, and recognised Him as the Son of Man who lived and died a year or two ago. And when we think of the charge that was brought against him ; when we think of some of the things that escaped his lips in the great defence, when we think of the words he spoke as he knelt under the rain of murderous stones, we cannot help feeling that he saw Jesus in the flesh once or twice at least. Was he among the company of Greeks that desired to see Jesus during that Passover week that ended in the Cross ? Philip was the disciple whom they approached, and the so-called early confusion of Philip the disciple with Philip the Evangelist may possibly be no confusion at all, but the truth. The disciple may have had a Greek connection, for his name is Greek, and though the committee of Seven were elected to relieve the Apostles, we are not thereby debarred from supposing that one of the Seven belonged to the band of Apostles. Philip who was a good calculator and had Greek sympathies, was probably doing a large share of the relief-work among the Hellenist widows, for whose sake the Seven were set apart. If there was to be continuity in the work the Seven would have to be guided and advised. And though Stephen was made convener, Philip,

who is named second, may have been a disciple
put on as consulting member. It is only his later
career, partly in the company of Stephen, that won
for him the title of " Evangelist." Nor does it seem
likely that two very prominent Christians of the
earliest days, each of them having virgin daughters,
and each named Philip, should have come to settle
in the same region in their closing years. The
friendship of Stephen and Philip might well date
from this striking episode in the career of Jesus—
the interview that certain Greeks had with Him.
For it was the attraction of the Prophet that had
drawn them, and Jesus seems to have thought He
had won some of them. He was elated by their
visit—as though they were to Him the first earnest
of a world-wide harvest (John xii. 32). However
the case may be, Stephen was surely in the Temple
courts on one of the first mornings of that Passion
week, when the Man from Galilee with the gentle,
holy bearing created an unlooked-for and tremendous
commotion. Suddenly with a whip of knotted cords
He strode into the midst of the trafficking, and in an
awful majesty of indignant wrath cleared the Court
of the desecrators, with their clamour of haggling
and bargaining ; upsetting their tables, and driving
them forth through the gates. We fancy we see
the young dreamer from the South arrested by this
action of the Dreamer from the Northern highland
Lake. We see him spell-bound, gathering in with
the humble folk to listen to His talk, and he heard
the Nazarene say of this sacred place which He named
His Father's House, that it was called a House of
Prayer for *all nations* ; nay, that one day not very
far away, this House was to be thrown down, and
that He was to build a new Temple, a spiritual

Temple, an unseen Temple not made with hands; and that in this Temple—anywhere and everywhere, where seeking souls lifted up praying hands in spirit and in truth—there was to be the true worship of the one God, the Infinite Spirit, the Father of all.

Why, it must have sounded like an answer to his prayers, like the beginning of the fulfilment of all his dreams. One day passed, and then another, and still the great new thoughts would keep lingering and growing in his mind. And then as he wandered through the crowded streets on the morning of Paschal eve he must have heard the mob shouting "Crucify, crucify!" And he followed to Calvary, crept close in horror to get a right look at the condemned man, and found that his fears were all too true. It was the Nazarene. He heard the nails being hammered through the hands. And from the lips he heard the anguished prayer escape: "Father, forgive them, for they know not what they do." . . . Crucified? He crucified? And dead? Clean gone for ever from the world? Oh, it cannot be true!

He had begun to build his hopes upon the Nazarene more strongly than he knew. With the terrible scene so burned in upon his soul, he must have gone for a time as one distracted, robbed, it would seem for ever, of his peace of mind. Perhaps peace came to him at Pentecost, when he heard Peter on the city street declare to the wondering crowd that this Man was the Messiah, and that He was risen from the dead. "It was not possible that He should be holden of death." There rose up before Stephen's vision the memory of the majestic Figure moving amid a tempest of excitement in the Temple courts, Himself wrapped in an air of unnatural sweetness and calm ; and his hungry heart clutched at the words. " No, no, it was not possible that a Personality so tremendous could be holden of death. It is true, it is true ! He is alive and at the right hand of God, and it is He, the same Mighty Personality that is moving in the heart of this Pentecost crowd to-day. His dream—His dream of the invisible Temple has begun to become fact to-day." " There is none other name under heaven given among men whereby we must be saved," the speaker was saying. Lifted on the wings of ecstasy, Stephen named this Jesus " Lord."

There can be no doubt about what followed. This young man's giving of himself to Christ was perfect and flawless, one of the most thorough and wholehearted surrenders and consecrations there has ever been. How could it be otherwise ? This Jesus with His mighty vision of the universal Father God and the world-wide Kingdom that was to be, was so obviously the answer to all his yearnings and dreams. It was the turning of the sun-flower to the Sun. Everybody saw and felt the change. Unmistakably the young man was a life dedicated and set apart. The writer of the book of Acts does his best to reproduce the general impression about him in varying phrase. The Apostles, when the problem arose which led to the appointing of the committee of Seven, said they wanted men " full of the Holy Spirit, and of wisdom " ; and Stephen was elected at the head of the poll. He was a man " full of faith," the writer says ; or—if we follow the reading of the best MSS.—the phrase is " full of grace." And he repeats it in other forms, so anxious is he to record aright what men thought of him : " full of the Holy Spirit," and again " full of

power." Men felt that the Unseen had laid hold
of him, had found in him a remarkable medium,
and used him in the most direct and impressive
way when he spoke. And this Christ-dedicated
soul began at once to give his testimony.

Where would he speak ? Where else but in the
little chapel, the synagogue of the colonists of the
South, whither he had resorted all his student days ?
The Jewish synagogue service was less formal, less
ceremonial, less dependent on a single official than
the acts of worship we are familiar with. Almost
anyone who had the gift and the education could speak
if he felt disposed. And in Jerusalem, where the
Temple services overshadowed everything, these
synagogues would be more of the nature of social
centres and discussion clubs. Probably the young
orator with the Greek culture had spoken there
with acceptance in his Judaistic days. But after
Christ won him, his old associates must have been
surprised and startled at the change. By-and-by
he began to say things that were very disconcerting.
They were taken aback, but their curiosity was
aroused. They let him speak and speak again.
Yes, there could be no mistaking it at length ; it
was rank heresy the young man was talking. And
soon all the Jewish congregations of Jerusalem were
chattering about him and his views, and the other
synagogue of Greek-speaking Jews—not so strict,
these colonials, as their Palestine compatriots—would
invite him to speak to them. And there was that
little thin-haired, sickly-faced fellow—the former
student from Tarsus—sitting in the audience.
They listened for a while complacently. By-and-by
a glitter of intolerant fury began to blaze out in
those eyes set in their swollen red lids, and there

were interruptions and arguments, and hot words—
in short, a scene. The young dreamer's searching
words had been like a sharp lance-point beginning
to probe the pride and prejudice of the Pharisaic
conscience of the young man from Tarsus. And his
first impulse was to strike out against it—like an ox.
The scales of prejudice were forced apart for an
instant, by the speaker's inexorable logic, and then
they closed tight shut. No doubt some listened
wonderingly and receptively in both synagogues,
but the most prejudiced and Law-hardened were
roused to resentment. And they kidnapped the
daring innovator and haled him before the Sanhedrin.
He was charged with speaking blasphemies against
Moses and against God. He had been speaking,
they said, against this Holy Place, and against the
Law. He had been daring to say that their day
was passing away : the old order was changing,
and a new and higher form of faith had come to
take its place ; that we Jews had made God too
narrow and exclusive ; that the Temple was not
the only place where God bestowed blessing ; that
God's true Temple was in any place where earnest
souls were led to pray.

And the High Priest said : "Young man, what
have you got to say for yourself ? Are these things
so ? " Then began one of the most subtle and
powerful pieces of special pleading conceivable.
When we study it, we can well imagine the effect of
it on a Jew, self-complacent in the fact that he
belonged to the chosen race, that he and his people
had access to God in a way that no one else had,
and that in fact the Temple at Jerusalem *was* the
only place where God revealed His true glory.
The young Stephen stands tearlessly confronting

the most imposing court of those who held that faith ; and this is what he says :

" I am a Jew. I believe in my people's past. But I will prove to you that you are wrong. When God appeared to Abraham at first, was it to Mount Zion that He came ? Abraham had never heard of Mount Zion. It was far away on the plains of Mesopotamia, where men worshipped the sun, moon, and stars. When Joseph was sold by the jealousy of his brothers, and carried to Egypt, was he carried beyond the presence of God ? Nay, ' God was with him.' When your forefathers were in Egyptian bondage, were they deprived of the presence and interest of God ? 'I have seen the affliction of my people,' God said to Moses. And where did God reveal Himself to Moses ? Mount Zion ? No, but on the lonely steppes among the sheep-flocks at the back of Horeb, in the peninsula of Sinai. And when your forefathers journeyed through the wilderness forty years, were they out of touch with God ? Nay, but the pillar and the cloud went with them night and day. And at Sinai, not Zion, Moses became mediator of the Law from God to His people. And the tent of witness moved with them from place to place in spite of their frequent disloyalty. And in the land of promise what happened ? Did our people always walk in the presence of God ? Why, they forsook Him, worshipped local Baals—yes, even in the Holy Land ! "

We can see that critical and excited assembly following him step by step, nodding grave approval at first, sure of themselves ; then becoming tense with apprehension as he began to come nearer home. And then at last he reached the climax of his argument :

" As for this House, this Holy Temple within whose walls we are now met, it was not till the days of Solomon that it was built. Did God cease to be the One God whose presence is everywhere when this Temple was built ? Did He gather and contract Himself, and confine Himself here ? What say our own holy prophets ? 'The Most High dwelleth not in temples made with hands.' ' Heaven is God's throne, the earth is His footstool. What house would you build me ? saith God.' "

Step by step the young orator had led his audience to this climax. And step by step he had felt the movement and consent of their minds growing slower and more reluctant ; until at last at this point, though the argument was irrefutable, never-the-less he became conscious that the mind of his audience had come to a dead halt, and stubbornly refused to move a step further. They may have interrupted here, but there is no indication of that, though we are told of the interruption a moment later. It was probably the orator's instinct that guided him as to the feeling of the listeners. They saw what was coming, and they were terrified. Stephen felt as if he had been driving an ox and waggon, and then this terrifying thing loomed in front, and the beast stopped, and the waggon came on, and the pole slid the yoke right up to the back of its ears, and the neck stretched—and stiffened ; not a step more would it budge. And then he applied the goad : " Ye stiff-necked, and uncircumcised in heart and ears, ye do always resist the Holy Spirit. . . ."

And then the clamour broke out, and in their fury they gnashed on him with their teeth. And there was a young man there in the crowd, standing on tip-toe to see over the shoulders of his neighbours, and his voice was the loudest of them all—kicking with the rest against the prick. And the young prisoner-at-the-bar stood facing them, fearlessness written on his handsome, god-like face. Nay, it had become all lighted and glowing with the rapture of the moment—that *he* should have been called to do and suffer this for Jesus, his Lord! What delusion! thought Saul; that " a cause so foul should so wear the brows of grace." And yet—and yet—? . . . As those serene, blue, far-off, dreaming eyes looked round on his accusers, perhaps they caught a glimpse of those other red, fiery and vindictive eyes looking over the shoulder of some haughty and disdainful Pharisee; and a message of recognition passed between the two; and Stephen's look was full of a mute, but eager appeal. And then he lifts his eyes upwards. Hark! What is he saying? "I see Jesus, the Son of Man, standing on the right hand of God." For an instant the memory of a despised felon on a cross flashed on Saul's vision. Then he thrust his fingers into his ears, like the rest of the crowd. And they rushed on the accused man and dragged him out and lynched him.

Surely we see the supreme importance of this young man's story in the divine economy of Providence. By that deed of his, and by his sacrifice, the Gospel truth was wrenched free for ever from the trammels of the past; for in a few weeks the hunted Christians who had scattered to Antioch and elsewhere, were proclaiming the message for the first time without any misgiving to the Gentiles. And it was from that Antioch Church that by-and-by the great world-mission was organised. But—crowning glory!—through this same episode the great persecutor came at last to be the great protagonist of the Cross. Stephen's death wrought into fact the truth he proclaimed.

Outside the city walls, where the martyr knelt amid the hurtling stones, this other fellow-student stood, consenting to his death, keeping the coats of those who did the dirty work. Why did he not join in himself ? Had the sword of the Spirit already begun to pierce and reach home to the heart of his pride ?—We wonder . . . And listen ! The lips of the dying man are moving. He is in spirit with Jesus in His agony ; he is remembering again the scene on Calvary, and hearing from the gentle lips the prayer breathed as they battered in the nails, " Father, forgive them, for they know not what they do." And following his Lord's example, he too prays, " Lord Jesus, lay not this sin to their charge."—Aye, *so* the Arch-deceiver Himself had died. No, not deceiving, but deluded ; no deceiver would suffer so for his word. . . . Deluded ? . . . Was He deluded ? . . .

From that hour the fate of Saul of Tarsus was sealed. For a few weeks he went like a madman, fighting against remorse of conscience, resisting furiously the haunting conviction that the dead Stephen was right and he was wrong ; keeping his questioning to himself, haling men and women to judgment ; kicking against the pricks still. For

> Who lights the faggot ?
> Not the full faith ; no, but the lurking doubt.

His expedition to Damascus has recently been described in memorable words : " Six days' ride from Jerusalem gate, with a clump of constables behind the Sheriff of the Sanhedrin. Six silent rides in that cloddish company ; lonely rides, but

The First Witness for Christian Liberty

is there One who rides at his bridle unperceived ? The debate goes on, insistent, truceless, tireless, without discharge. The question pursues him, masterful, merciless, a tyrant o'er a slave, a ghost behind the haunted, till the haunted seems a ghost to his own self." At last as the long journey drew to an end, his restless soul, fretting against the tedium of the way, tired of the long debate within, sank into a horror of darkness. He was lost ! All that he had stood for so rigidly in the past had failed him. And through the darkness he seemed to hear the roar of an angry crowd, and a voice that cried, as though some angel's heart had been riven through with sudden sorrow, " Lord Jesus, lay not this sin to their charge." And then behind the tumult loomed the shadow of a Cross. " Accursèd tree ! Execrable death ! " his pride kept saying ; but his conscience answered, " Who cursed it ? Who made it cursèd ? You and your people's sin ! "

Then suddenly the spiritual darkness was rent, and the light leapt into his soul—dawnlight, morning light, broad day, flooding in more and more, until he flung himself to earth, for it had grown brighter than the noonday sun. " Saul, Saul," he heard the Voice that he had once scorned declare—" Saul, Saul, why persecutest thou me ? " " Who art thou, Lord ? " But he needed not to ask, for already he had said " Lord." " I am Jesus, whom thou persecutest It is hard for thee to kick against the pricks." . . . " Lord, what wilt thou have me to do ? "

O Saul,

> Then flashed it on thy spirit mightily,
> That thou hadst spurned a love that died for thee ;
> And all thy pride went down in whelming flood
> Of boundless shame, and boundless gratitude.

CHAPTER V

The House of Alphai

THOSE who are not interested in genealogies may
well skip this chapter. It is with the family connections of some of the personalities that surrounded
our Lord that we are to be mainly concerned.
Certainty of course cannot be claimed for the
identifications here made. But the facts cohere
and seem to be a possible avenue of insight into
the beginnings of the Jewish Christian Church in
Jerusalem.

To write a true and intimate history of any
family, it would be necessary to know the family
fictions and prejudices as well as the family facts.
For it is in the light of these we see the family ideal.
And the clue to the history of the House of Alphai
seems to us to lie in its tendency to be unduly
impressed with the importance of ceremonial and
traditional observance. According to Jeremiah,
"Thus saith the LORD, Stand ye in the ways, and see,
and ask for the old paths, where is the good way, and
walk therein, and ye shall find rest for your souls."
Religious conservatism has its place, no doubt.
Its good and its bad side are exemplified in this
family's history. If we keep this fact in mind, we
may possibly find that this chronicle is not without
its ethical and religious value.

It was a great day in the history of the House
of Alphai when the Saviour of the world walked

The House of Alphai

up to the customs-desk in Capernaum and whispered to Levi " Follow me." The capture of Levi by Jesus was probably the beginning of this family's religious glory. They all seem to have become followers of Jesus. And it was the reclaiming of Matthew that doubtless led to the winning of the rest.

Levi, or Matthew, is the best known of the group. It was the supreme moment of his life when he was called from an outwardly important position, chief customs-house officer at this great toll-house on the *Via Maris ;* laid aside his ponderous ledger-rolls ; and as the devotee of the Galilean Prophet went up along the road that led to the ignominy of a Cross. It seemed like courting oblivion and disgrace. Yet really, as we now see, it meant becoming a shining star among those who have done most for the spiritual welfare of the world. He was fond of making notes, and from jotting down figures, he took to jotting down many of the golden words which fell from the lips of the Master, into a journal which is now enshrined in the Gospel that bears his name.

Papias says Matthew made a written collection of the Logia (Sayings) in the Hebrew (Aramaic) dialect. And Irenæus says he did it among the Hebrews (that is, in Palestine), about the time of the activities of Peter and Paul in Rome. Origen explains that it was given out to those who had transferred their faith from Judaism. Eusebius declares it was after he had first preached to them, and when he was about to go elsewhere. But it was not the Gospel as we now have it that came from Matthew's pen. Our Gospel is a compilation in which Mark's is incorporated in large measure. Yet there is no reason for doubting that the long groups of Sayings came from Matthew's journal. And since the Gospel as we now know it was compiled soon after the fall of Jerusalem at the latest, and still retains the Jewish outlook—the reverence for the Law, the leanings to Old Testament prophecy, the conception of Christ as Messiah who was to return soon, the conception of His ingathered Kingdom as an enlarged and purified Chosen People, it has doubtless emanated from the Jewish Christian Church in Palestine. And the compiler was some one who had access to Matthew's journal, one of the circle of Matthew's friends in fact. For we seem to find the impression of Matthew's personality in the Gospel as well as the Logia. Is it wholly beyond the bounds of possibility that Matthew himself compiled the first edition of it, translating his own journal from the Aramaic to make it correspond with his incorporations from Mark? His position as frontier customs-house officer surely implies that he understood Greek.

The man himself is almost lost behind the pages of the journal. Yet not wholly so. All the synoptic Gospels tell of the decisive nature of his experience. He made a complete and sudden break with his past, when he " rose and followed." And when Luke assures us that it was Levi who made the feast that ensued, there is no reason to doubt that he correctly interprets Mark's ambiguous phrase after the story of the call—" *his* house." This feast to honour Christ was a noble way of confessing the change in his life. The best explanation he could offer of his action was to let Christ be seen and heard by his old associates. There is a self-effacement here which the journal enshrined in the first Gospel corroborates. It consists almost entirely of the great life-giving words of his Lord. When we compare it with the second Gospel, which consists of Peter's reminiscences of the immortal story, we see at once how completely the man has hidden himself. If, indeed, any disciple is magnified in the first Gospel it is Peter again.

But his candour also we must not overlook. It seems to us to be due to Matthew that the kindly reticence of Mark and Luke is overcome in the first Gospel. For there, Matthew is not called the son of Alphai on the occasion of his call. A man does not usually speak of himself as the son of so-and-so when he writes about himself. At any rate the omission is not due to the fact that Alphai was unknown to the readers of the first Gospel, for he is named in the list of disciples as the father of the second James soon after (x. 3)—and named without qualification as though he were quite well-known. But the much more important fact about the telling of the story of the call in the first Gospel is that the name given is Matthew. In the other Gospels the name is Levi, with never a hint that this is Matthew the disciple.

And when we proceed to an examination of the list of the Twelve given in this Gospel, there are certain features about it which suggest that the hand of an eye-witness has been at work on Mark's somewhat less precise recollections of what he heard from Peter. It is no slavish copy. It omits the reference to the " sons of thunder ": such a by-name would be of greater interest to Peter, who was more closely associated with these two brothers than Matthew or his friends. But the two most interesting deviations from Mark's arrangement have each something of value to add to our delineation of the man. The list is given at a different point in the narrative from Mark's—at the time of the sending out of the disciples ; and they are arranged in a different order and in pairs. It is surely a disciple's recollection of Jesus' arrangement when He sent them out two by two. It couples Andrew with Peter, and mentions that he is his brother. They would naturally go out together ; so would the sons of Zabdai, who follow. The coupling of Philip with Bartholomew (bar-Tolmai " son of brotherliness "—perhaps a name given by Jesus) reminds us of the friendship of Philip and Nathanael, recorded in the Fourth Gospel. Jesus would naturally send these two friends out together ; as He would similarly the last pair on the list, Simon the Canaanean and Judas Iscariot, kindred spirits, for whose kinship by blood a strong case can be made out.

But our interest centres rather in the remaining four, and particularly Thomas and Matthew. One tradition would apparently make Thomas a brother of Matthew, but probably it was the divine wisdom of Jesus that associated them. Thomas the brooder would need an associate who had had a clear-cut religious experience ; a large-hearted, good-natured companion, who would be patient with his doubts. There is some evidence for believing that Thomas' original name was Judas. Thomas (the " twin ") is obviously a cognomen. Jesus was fond of these love-names for His disciples. One of the Judases had two by-names : Lebbai (hearty), perhaps to distinguish him from the cold-blooded " man of Kerioth " ; and Thaddai (lively). " Hearty " was not the right word to distinguish him from " the twin," who was warm-hearted too (John xi. 16).

The House of Alphai

So when Jesus found him in the company of the
" twin," and wanted to address anything specially
to him, he would use the kindred word with somewhat different significance—" Thaddai " (lively—
perhaps " jolly " in the Mark Tapley sense of
" courageously optimistic "), for " the twin " was
melancholy. Why was Thomas called " twin " ?
There would be little point in the cognomen if his
twin brother were outside the band, and on the other
hand it would be no distinguishing mark if his twin
brother were among the Twelve. Of course, if his
name were Judas, it did distinguish him from the
other two. But that alone could not have been
the reason for the appellation. Did he perhaps
cling to Matthew like his shadow, because he found
in him that which was lacking in his own nature ?
Was there perhaps some odd resemblance in their
features also ?

But the character of Matthew, as seen against
the counterfoil of Thomas' temperament, can be
seen *directly* in this list as well. In this Gospel
alone, as we saw, is he called Matthew in the story
of his call. And now in the list, as if purposely
reiterating the fact, in order that we may make no
mistake about it, he is called " Matthew *the* tax-
gatherer." Mark and Luke give the name Levi
when they tell about his call. Mark does not even
call him tax-gatherer (execrable name to a Jew),
but gently refers to him as " sitting at the receipt
of custom." And Luke only gets the length of
naming him " a tax-gatherer called Levi." Does
it not sound as if here in the list in the first Gospel
we were listening to Matthew himself taking pains
to secure that we shall be under no delusions as to
his identity. Once more the candour of the man

is apparent. Although a disciple, he does not claim to be anything more than the reclaimed tax-gatherer.

Large-hearted the man must have been also. In that feast in his house, his compassionate sympathy with the under-dog is obvious in the character of the guests. It must have been a supreme joy to him to record Christ's defence of the outcasts. And it must have been a supreme joy to Jesus that at last He had reached those whom He sought— " the lost sheep of the House of Israel "—through this notable conquest. The reiteration of that phrase in this Gospel looks like a reflection of Matthew's attitude. It must have been a word often on the lips of this disciple, who gave himself to proclaiming the Gospel in his native land. " Matthew " must have been Jesus' name for him. Levi, the tax-gatherer, became " the gift of God " to Jesus. One fancies, too, from this same trait of his, that Levi had never been happy in the tax-gathering business. Outcasts are fain to club together in a fraternity of wretchedness, and his obvious fellow-feeling for his old associates shows that he felt the ostracism keenly. Doubtless he was sensitive by nature, and had been drawn to listen to Jesus through this very wretchedness of soul. One thinks of the hymn :

> Souls of men, why will ye scatter
> Like a crowd of frightened sheep ?

when one thinks of Matthew. Something like it must have been the burden of his message to his fellow-countrymen.

It might be making words carry too great a weight to suggest that it is his modesty that has caused his own name to be placed *after* Thomas in the list. But it may not be without significance, that this position brings it next to James, the son of Alphai. Obviously it is to distinguish him from James the son of Zabdai that this James is so named in all the lists (Matt x. 3 ; Mark iii. 18 ; Luke vi 15 ; Acts i. 13). And this very method of distinguishing makes it practically certain that the second James was a Caperniote, like the sons of Zabdai. But Matthew was a Caperniote too, and only a little earlier in Mark's Gospel Matthew is named the son of Alphai. If the father of James were a different man, that could not but be mentioned here ; for no reader of the Gospel could fail to remember that Matthew was also a son of a man of that name. It is difficult to hold any other view than that Matthew and James were brothers, and tradition has it that James had been another tax-collector ; he had followed his brother's example. Beyond this we know next to nothing about James. There is but one fact apparent in the records. Of the three groups of four into which the disciples are divided, he is placed at the head of the last group in every list. He was the leader among the minor disciples. We can detect a general distinguishing characteristic between the three groups. The first group are the strong souls, whose inner life moves out and captures and dominates the outer life ; the heroic souls who have mastered themselves, and thereby won mastery over the world. In the second group there is a constant discord and strife between the outer and the inner life—Philip, the hesitator between outward fact and inward conviction ; Thomas, the brooder, torn between inner doubts and outer loyalties ; Nathanael or Bar-tolmai, divided between ancient prejudices and dreams of future glories ; Matthew, candid about his past and yet sensitive in the face of public opinion. The last group consists of those in whom there is no discord, because they live almost wholly on the outer surface of the soul. There are the Canaanean and Iscariot, obsessed by the idea of outward material and political power; and James and James' Judas—also surface minds. It was Judas, not Iscariot, who asked why Jesus was not to manifest Himself to the *world*. James, son of Alphai, was probably, therefore, one who had just drifted with the outer stream of life, drifted into the tax-collecting business and not thought very much about it. A man had to live; and if the Romans were in possession of the land, there was no use fighting against facts. Someone must do the tax-gathering, and why not he? What was the use of worrying about it like Matthew? Matthew was always querulous when he came in to see him, always with a new catalogue of slights and grievances. Until that memorable night when he called, his face all smiles, and said, "I am giving a feast to-night, will you come?" That was the end of the tax-collecting for James. He was one of those lost things that the Master had talked about that night at Matthew's feast. Lost—and found!

Who then was Alphai, the father of these men? Almost all that we can affirm of him is that he too must have become a follower of Jesus. He is always spoken of as one well-known to the early Christians. Peter, to whom the reminiscences in the second Gospel are due, speaks of him familiarly. He was a fellow-townsman of his in all probability. But his mention in the first Gospel shows that he was not unknown to the Jerusalem Christians. Possibly he was a trader, or merchant, for out of this class we may suppose the tax-gatherers were drawn. It may be a reflection of his keenness in a worldly sense, that no less than two of his sons had entered the hated profession. The passion for wealth gives a kind of spurious courage to face obloquy. This prosperous man had possibly followed his sons when they went to Jerusalem to become propagandists of the new faith. He may have set up business again in the Holy City, and so may have taken an active share in the doings of the Jerusalem Christians. A father who had two sons in the disciple-band must have been held in high esteem by the Church of the beginning.

But that is not all the glory of Alphai. Luke alone among the synoptists speaks of a " Judas of James " in the band (Luke vi. 16 ; Acts i. 13). He stands in the place which Lebbai or Thaddai occupies in the others. The Fourth Gospel corroborates the fact that there was a " Judas, not Iscariot " among the disciples (John xiv. 22). Doubtless this Judas is the twice by-named disciple. The phrase, " Judas of James " has been wrongly translated " Judas the brother of James," on the supposition that the James in question is the brother of our Lord, and that this Judas is identical with the writer of the Epistle of Jude, who calls himself " the brother of James." Joses (Mark xv. 40) and Simon the Zêlot are added to the band of brothers, and their father is said to be the brother of Joseph the carpenter of Nazareth. These are the names of the so-called brothers of Jesus, and the theory is that they are only cousins. The whole theory, laden with improbabilities, has been invented in the interests of a dogma of the perpetual virginity of Jesus' mother ; and must be set aside.

The phrase can only mean " Judas, son of James."

And it cannot mean the son of the son of Zabdai, any more than it can mean the brother of the brother of our Lord. He is named just after a James, and if it were any other James who was his father, some distinguishing mark would have been added to this third-mentioned James in the list. Judas, not Iscariot, is the son of the son of Alphai.

The mention of Joses (some MSS. of high authority read " Joseph ") a moment ago, suggests another path to pursue in this enquiry into the relationships of the House of Alphai. Among the ministering women who stood looking on at the Crucifixion (Mark xv. 40f.; Matt. xxvii. 55f.; *cf.* Luke viii. 3, xxiii. 49, 55f), and who came to the garden of the sepulchre (Mark xv. 47, xvi. 1; Matt. xxvii. 61, xxviii. 1; Luke xxiv. 10), mention is made of " Mary, the mother of James the Little, and of Joses." Sometimes she is called " Mary, the mother of James" (Mark xvi. 1), sometimes "Mary, the mother of Joses " (Mark xv. 47), sometimes merely " the other Mary " (Matt. xxvii. 61, xxviii. 1). James and Joses are evidently well-known Christians in the early Church. Can we identify them ? From the use of the phrase in Mark's Gospel, Peter was evidently in the habit of referring to one of the well-known Jameses in the early Church as " James the Little." It probably has reference to physical stature, not to importance among the first followers of Jesus. But, though our Bible has wrongly translated it " the Less," yet the epithet is meant as a distinguishing mark. We may be certain it is not Zabdai's son who is referred to, because Salome who follows (in one list) is described (in another) as the mother of Zabdai's sons. We may be almost equally certain it is not the brother of Jesus who is meant. That

fact—of kinship with Jesus—would have been used
as distinguishing mark (*cf.* Gal. i. 19); indeed,
their mother would have been called the mother
of Jesus. Further, it is used as the distinguishing
mark of a member of a company in which there
were more than one of that name. James, the
brother of Jesus, was *not* one of the disciples. The
family disbelieved in Jesus—were estranged from
Him during the days of His flesh. And afterwards
the brethren of the Lord (Acts i. 14, xii. 17; 1 Cor.
ix. 5), and expressly James (Acts xv. 13; 1 Cor.
xv. 7; Gal. i. 19),—although in the letter to Galatia
he gets the title "Apostle,"—are distinguished from
the disciples. Now in the New Testament there
is no other group with two Jameses except the
disciples. Most probably therefore James the Little
is the second James of the disciple circle—James the
son of Alphai. That Mary was the mother of
Matthew is never asserted, but it is precarious to
argue from silence; and indeed Matthew may have
been a son of a former wife of Alphai.

The Fourth Gospel, however, seems to set difficulties in the way of accepting this reading of the
facts. The writer tells us that "there stood by
the Cross of Jesus His mother, and His mother's
sister, Mary of Klopas, and Mary Magdalene"
(John xix. 25). At first sight it might seem that
Mary of Klopas was the sister of Jesus' mother.
But that there should be two Marys in one family
is a very improbable circumstance. And when we
turn to the synoptic list of women, where Jesus'
mother is not mentioned, there are three names—
Salome, wife of Zabdai, Mary the mother of James
and Joses, and Mary Magdalene. So that, besides
the mother, the Fourth Gospel probably thinks

of three other women, and the same three as the
synoptists do ; thus Jesus' mother's sister is Salome
of Zabdai. May it not be the delicacy of John,
the authority behind the Fourth Gospel, that has
withheld the name of his mother ? But it follows
also that Mary of Klopas is probably the mother of
James and Joses.

Here, however, another difficulty confronts us.
If James the Little is the son of Alphai, then Alphai
is the husband of Mary. The difficulty is not
insuperable. That 'Alphai when it is Græcised
becomes Kôlpa, and then by a common trans-
position, Klôpa is maintained by more than one
linguistic scholar. Another view is that " Mary of
Klopa" means " Mary the daughter of Klopa."
Hegesippus says that Klopa was the brother of
Joseph the carpenter. This would make Mary the
cousin of Jesus. But even so, it is not impossible
that a son and grandson of hers might be in the
disciple circle. It does not seem possible, however,
to identify Klopas with Kleopas, one of the two
who had the wonderful experience on the road to
Emmaus. The names are quite different ; and Alphai
belonged to Capernaum most probably, not to
Emmaus. For Mary was one of the ministering
women who followed Jesus from Galilee (Mark
xv. 41). That she was a woman of substance
supports our view of the prosperity of Alphai.

If our identifications are correct, the family tree of
the House of Alphai might be set down as follows :

Alphai (Klôpas ?)==Mary

Matthew (Levi) (disciple).	Joses (not a disciple).	James the Little (disciple).
		Judas (disciple).

The House of Alphai

The secret of this family's story, and of the part they played in the early Church, lies, we have said, in the family prejudice, the family observance of convention. It may be that men who have been guided long by the rigid rule of figures tend to become legalists in their moral outlook. But whether it be so in this case or not, what we know of the mother Mary would lead us to suppose her mind was governed by a sense of the importance of convention and ceremony. She was one of the women who watched the Crucifixion. Even when she learned that Jesus had been fitly buried, she came with the Magdalene to identify the site of the grave ; for she and her companion had determined that they would risk anything in order to perform the last tender offices of love for the dead body of their Lord. It was the promptings of woman's devoted love, no doubt,—and love spending itself, as it is always fain to do, in carrying out the minutest details of the funeral offices. But amid the terror of these days of darkness, love might well be content to know that the Loved One had been decently laid to rest in a proper grave. Yet with infinite courage she resolved to accept the grave risk, that the last punctilio might be performed. It may be that it is her forceful personality that impressed itself so strongly on the other members of the family. Let us try to follow the fortunes of some of them a little further.

The legalistic tendencies of Matthew are apparent in the Gospel which bears his name. He preserved the oracles of the Lord apparently in the fond hope that they would become the laws of the New Covenant. And his reverence for the ancient Law is apparent there also. It is said indeed that in later years he became an ascetic, living on "seeds and nuts and herbs, without flesh" (Clem. Al. *Pedag.*, II. i. 16). But it is certain he remained a noble monument to the power of the spirit of Christ, spending himself and being spent in labours for the Master's cause among the people of his own land, and possibly even in wider fields. Whether his end was martyrdom, as tradition sometimes affirms, or otherwise, he doubtless remained true till death to the Lord, who had said to him at the toll-desk, " Follow me."

A less happy fate seems to have been reserved for the other members of the family. The suicide of Judas of Kerioth made a vacancy in the disciple band, which the eleven proceeded to fill when they rallied after the Cross. They laid down as a condition for candidature that the nominees must be from those " who have kept company with us all the time that the Lord Jesus went in and out among us " from the beginning, and witnesses to the resurrection (Acts i. 21f.). The unsuccessful one among those selected as a short leet is named Joseph bar-Sabbas (another reading gives Joses ; apparently the forms are interchangeable), also called Justus.

It is quite clear from the Synoptic Gospels that Joses, the son of Mary and Alphai, was a well-known figure in the early Church, better known than his mother, since she is distinguished by reference to him. Probably too he was a follower of Jesus from the days of the beginning. Is there anything to forbid the suggestion that the Joses of the Gospels is the Joseph of the short leet ? " Bar-Sabbas " suggests at first sight a difficulty. It seems to mean " son of Sabba." But the best texts spell the word with a double " b," which means most likely that this is a cognomen signifying " Son of the Sabbath."

The House of Alphai

Such a name was sometimes added to that of a child born on the Sabbath day. But perhaps we may be permitted to discern in the title "Justus," although it is a name commonly enough adopted among Jews, another explanation. It might be interpreted as the Latin equivalent of the Greek word used to describe a punctilious observer of the ceremonial law. And there was evidently a strong section in the Jerusalem early Church who were inclined that way. They dominated the congregation by-and-by. The head of the community, James, the Lord's brother, became known as "the Just." And we know from *The Acts* and from Paul's letters, of the crisis that arose over the admission of the Gentiles. Now one of the very earliest points of contention in Jerusalem must certainly have been about the ceremonial observance of the old Jewish Sabbath. Were the Christians to continue attending synagogue worship? We know that they did at first (Acts iii. 1). We have no account of the time when the first day of the week became the Christian day of worship, though at the time of Paul's last journey to Jerusalem we read of him meeting with the Christians at Troas on the first day of the week for the breaking of bread (Acts xx. 7). But it is certain that after the martyrdom of Stephen the question of breaking absolutely with the ancient religious *régime* of Israel must have become acute. Those who fled from Jerusalem at that time were those who took Stephen's view of it. Those who remained were the ones least liable to persecution, since they favoured adherence to the old; and one who took a leading part in the agitation for abiding by the ancient ceremonial may well have been called " bar-Sabbas "—a leader of the Sabbath party.

In any case the name is not a patronymic, and does not militate against the suggestion that Joseph bar-Sabbas is Joses, the son of Alphai and Mary. The concern for strict ceremonial which was a trait of Mary, may have been reproduced in the son. At any rate the Joses mentioned in the Gospels was probably a follower of Jesus from the beginning—Eusebius says he was one of the Seventy—so that there is every likelihood that all the conditions laid down as necessary for membership in the disciple-band are fulfilled in Joses. And we are told of no other Joses who fulfils these requirements. Jesus' brother of that name is ruled out, since he doubtless joined with the family in discrediting Jesus when the family estrangement took place. Joseph of Arimathæa does not fulfil the conditions, since he only joined the disciples after Calvary. Joseph Barnabas, who must not be confused with this man (the name is quite different), evidently did not become a full disciple till Pentecost, though he may have come in contact with Jesus before the Cross. And he became a Gentile missionary, not a Judaising Christian of Jerusalem.

So Joseph bar-Sabbas, who began well as a devoted follower of Jesus, who was privileged to share the Resurrection experiences, seems to have been fated always to fail to rise to the height of his great calling. There is a pathos about his frequent disappointments. He had not to the full measure the all-or-nothing Christ-spirit. Jesus did not fully trust him. He was not called to be a disciple. And though nominated by the rest of the disciples for the vacant place in later days, yet the lot passed him by. Perhaps there was a touch of the bitterness of disappointment about his " Sabbath " agitation ;

perhaps he was one of those who followed Paul's foot-steps trying to undo his work. Paul does sometimes speak of one in particular, who, in his opposition, claimed greater privileges of fellowship with Christ than he. In the letter to the Galatians (according to the best MSS.) we are told about a certain man coming to Antioch, professedly from James the brother of the Lord, and destroying the harmonious fellowship between Peter and the Gentile Christians (Gal. ii. 12, cf. v. 10). When the Judaisers followed Paul to Corinth, they seem to have borne commenda-tory letters from the Church in Jerusalem; and they claimed to derive their authority from the Apostles. As events proved, Paul was really God's nominee for the vacant place among the Twelve. And often a defeated aspirant shows a certain dog-in-the-mangerism. We can feel the sting of Paul's sarcasm about the self-commenders in the letter to Corinth (2 Cor. x. 18). But one would fain think that Joses moderated his Judaistic tendencies by-and-by. It may be a calumny to suggest that he was ever one of the Judaisers whom Paul complains about. There is, in the letter to Colossæ (iv. 11), mention of one Jesus, surnamed Justus, who belonged to the cir-cumcision. One ancient document at least identifies him with Joses Justus. And Paul says that he and Mark (so we probably should limit the description) were the only ones of the circumcision who had been a comfort to him. The association may be signifi-cant. The unusual word for comfort means that which allays irritation. Mark, too, after proving unworthy, redeemed his reputation later. But the identification of this man with Joses Justus is very problematic. We like to think, however, that the story which Eusebius records of Joses bar-Sabbas who was also called Justus, is spiritually true at least : " A wonderful event happened respecting Justus surnamed bar-Sabbas, who though he drank deadly poison, experienced nothing injurious, by the grace of God " (Eus. *H. E.* III., 39). It was an early incident in the history of the Church; it is probably referred to in Mark (xvi. 18).

We have, as we think, one other chapter to record in the history of the House of Alphai. When the dispute between Jewish and Gentile Christianity came to a head in Jerusalem, the Assembly or Council convened to deal with the matter resolved to send a deputation to Antioch to convey their finding to the brethren. This deputation consisted of *Judas bar-Sabbas* and the prophet Silas (Acts xv. 22). Now we may be quite sure that in such a delicate matter the Council would take pains to secure that the deputation to be chosen should fulfil two requirements. The mission was one of conciliation; the decision of the Council was partly of the nature of a compromise. It should be conveyed to the Gentile community by men representative of both sides in the Jerusalem Church. But further, they should be men of such position and influence that the Antiochean Christians should have no cause to complain of discourtesy.

Now the two types of religious outlook which had come into collision were, on the one hand, those who laid all the emphasis on the side of spiritual experience, and, on the other, those who had strong leanings to ceremonial and legal observance. There can be no doubt as to which of these parties Silas represented. He belonged to those who trusted the warm and living manifestation and operation of the Spirit of God among believers. He himself had the *charisma*, or spiritual gift of utterance ; so much so that the Montanists—those ecstatics who sprang up in the second century—reckoned Silas a progenitor of their sect. It is natural to expect, therefore, in his fellow-deputy, a representative of the other party. It is true that Judas is called a prophet as well as Silas (Acts xv. 32). But the different ministeries of the Spirit were not sharply marked off from each other at this early date. Paul, for example, was not only an Apostle, but a prophet, a teacher, a healer. So that Judas' gift of exhortation does not preclude us from supposing that he had Judaistic leanings. For again notice the cognomen — " bar-Sabbas " (son of the Sabbath). Here, surely is another member of the party that would fain cling to the ancient ceremonies of Israel, and preserve Israel's holy day.

But who was this Judas bar-Sabbas ? The other requirement which the deputation had to fulfil was that its members must be " chief men among the brethren " (Acts xv. 22). They were men of position and authority. Silas as a prophet, ranked next in spiritual status to the Apostles. He is said to have been one of the Seventy. It is even possible that he received the title " Apostle " (1 Thess ii. 6) —one of those who had " seen the Lord." So that it is more than likely that he had followed Jesus when He lived on earth. But must not the other be of equal rank and dignity, seeing that the Judaistic party were so strong in Jerusalem ? Nay, should we not expect that, if the courtesies are to be fully observed in such an important and delicate mission, one of the deputation should, if at all possible, be an actual disciple of Jesus ? Only so would the proprieties be fully satisfied. There are no real grounds for assuming that all the disciples except Peter were absent from Jerusalem at this time. Was Judas bar-Sabbas, perchance, an Apostle in this sense ? It is surely significant that he is named first, each time the deputation is mentioned (Acts xv, 22, 27, 32). And then, further, as Luke's narrative informs us, " It pleased the *Apostles* and elders . . . to send chosen men of their own company " (Acts xv. 22). Must not the word " Apostles " be taken seriously here ? Now there was a Judas still among the Twelve, very possibly the youngest of the Apostles, for he is called " Judas, son of James," who, as we have seen reason to believe, was the second James mentioned in the lists of the Twelve. And the suggestive fact is that it is Luke only who tells us the name *was* Judas. The other Gospels only give him his by-name. The designations which Luke applies to the figures which flit across the pages of his history are always significant, and it may be that his careful naming of this Apostle (Acts i. 13) has a proleptic reference. May not this be he ? From what we know of him, he would be a very suitable member for this deputation. He was a man of courage and vivacity, as his by-names indicate. And no doubt at this very time he was one of the most energetic of the men of weight— at the very summit of his powers—in Jerusalem. The one reference to him in the Fourth Gospel gives us a clear hint as to the direction in which his thinking ran. " Lord," said Judas (not Iscariot) " Why is it that you are to appear to us and not to the world ? " After all Jesus' teaching of the Twelve, he was still looking for a public manifestation of the Messiah to the world, through the Chosen People. It was one of the conceptions which dominated the early Jewish Church in Palestine. It is all of a piece with our interpretation of the cognomen "bar-Sabbas." But although a strenuous advocate of the Jewish point of view, his temperament was such as to make him acceptable to the Christians of Antioch.

If the family tree which we have traced is correct, this disciple Judas was the nephew of Joses, son of Mary and Alphai. And the cognomen which we find attached to both of them—"bar-Sabbas"—becomes extremely suggestive. Uncle and nephew were among the chief advocates on the conservative side of the agitation concerning the ancient *régime* of the Jewish Sabbath,—closely allied indeed as leaders of the Sabbath party. The trait which we discovered in the mother of the family of Alphai has repeated itself in a son and a grandson. Yet the younger man had the broader mind. He must have been in favour of the policy of conciliation which the Council had decided to pursue. And the arrangement whereby he became one of the deputation is not without its personal interest. He was sent to allay the strife which the extreme Judaisers, whoever they were, had raised in Antioch and Jerusalem. If Joses had been active on the extreme side of that agitation, it is a moving thing to see the nephew going down to heal the division which the uncle had helped to bring about. It is a touching family atonement. After storms and separations, bitterness and cavilling, the House of Alphai—this nucleus of the Jewish party in the early Church in Jerusalem—remained true in the end to the Spirit of the Lord, whom they had followed so devotedly while He lived among men.

CHAPTER VI

"A Man—A Certain Macedonian"

THERE were Christians in Rome before the Apostle
of the Gentiles brought the Cross to Europe in the
autumn of 50 A.D., but this was the first great
Christian campaign on European soil. The story
of the modest soul whose pleading induced St. Paul
to cross the Ægean for the first time, ought to have
an abiding interest for us. And it is to it we now
would turn.

Some miles inland from the northern shore of
the Ægean Sea, there was, at the time of which we
speak, a town occupying a commanding site on the
rocky slopes of a steep hill. To the West lay a broad
plain called Drama, through which ran a many-
tributaried river. On the East lay a pass through
the mountains, leading towards the shores of the
Hellespont. Through the town passed a famous
Roman road—the *Via Egnatia*—which connected
Dyrrachium on the Adriatic with the Hellespont.
It was probably the greatest artery of travel and
commerce in the Roman Empire—this busy thorough-
fare which linked the East with the West. The
ancient name of the town was *Krēnides*, the place
of the streams or fountains. Philip of Macedon,
in whose territory it lay, had made it a flourishing
place and given it his own name. And in its subsequent history it was Philippi—Philip's town.

"A Man—A Certain Macedonian"

When the young Roman Emperor Augustus defeated the revolutionaries Brutus and Cassius on the plains of Drama near by, in the year 42 B.C., he settled a number of discharged Italian soldiers here in Philippi, and gave the place the special privileges of a *colonia*. It seems likely that these discharged army men got certain rights to property and soil. It was now ninety-two years after the battle. The Italian colonists had settled down and some of the families had grown prosperous. There is a strong presumption that the two brothers round whom our story centres were descended from one of these colonists from Italy, and that their family had achieved a comfortable position in the place.

One of the marked features of the life of this town was its interest in religion. The rocks near the ancient site of Philippi are strewn with ruins and relics of religious worship. There are traces of a temple of a Roman god Silvanus—the god of the frontiers—one of the most popular deities of the Roman Imperialistic party. It was probably built, therefore, by these colonist soldiers of the Emperor. There are traces of the worship of an Eastern deity—Mên. But the chief religion of the district was the worship of Dionysus. In the neighbouring mountains was "the most revered of his sanctuaries." It is a fact full of infinite pathos that the main feature of that religion was a festival in which was enshrined a story or myth of the god dying and rising again from the dead. As it appeared in the mystery religions, the initiates who took part in the rites were supposed to enter into communion with the god and share his dying and resurrection. All over the heathen world in that day the great religious longing was the longing for redemption from the futility and corruption, the essential evil of life. In this as in similar myths of the mystery-faiths, we see the great world stirring in its sleep of paganism, and dreaming uneasy dreams—dreams born of its deep desire—for a Redeemer. It should awaken no fear in us for the truth of our faith, to be reminded of these. On the contrary. " If," says G. K. Chesterton, " the Christian God really made the human race, would not the human race tend to rumours and perversions of the Christian God ? If the centre of our life is a certain fact, would not people far from the centre have a muddled version of that fact ? If we are so made that a Son of God must deliver us, is it odd that (pagans) should dream of a Son of God ? " Nothing is clearer than their dreaming of His drawing near, and their sense of the need of Him. The poet Aratos, who was educated at Tarsus, the home of St. Paul, lived some generations before this time. It was at the instigation of a Macedonian king that he wrote his great poem. And in it occur these touching lines, from which Paul once quoted a fragment :

> All the ways are full of God,
> All the gathering-places of men, the sea, and harbours,
> And at every turn we are all in need of God,
> For we are all of kin to him.

A cult which flourished in Thessaly, the neighbour-ing province, has a special interest for our story—the worship of Asklēpios, the god of healing, the saviour god who called all men to himself. For one of the two brothers round whom our story centres —the one we are most interested in—was a man whose heart was full of a deep pity for the multitudes of diseased and broken folk of whom the world around him was so full.

"A Man—A Certain Macedonian"

As these two brothers lived and moved in the streets of Philippi, they too must have been filled with all the vague but deep and irrepressible dreams and longings of the human soul which were the special mark of the time. By-and-by their family left the city, and seems, as we shall find reason for thinking, to have settled in a city on the borders between Phrygia and Pisidia. It was a fateful change for them, for soon a new faith was to spread like fire through all the valleys of Phrygia and Asia. Here they met Paul and his companions, and the new faith to which they listened—not a myth, but a great living fact—of One who was indeed a Healer and Saviour, One who died on a Cross and rose again, One who called God His Father, and revealed Him as a God of compassion and pity, longing to rescue all broken and blinded and sin-bound souls—was so exactly the answer to all their hitherto unsatisfied yearnings and questionings, that they were straightway won for Christ. It seems to have been on St. Paul's first missionary journey that all this took place, and indeed they must have been among his earliest converts ; for the tour of the island of Cyprus, save for the winning of Sergius Paulus, yielded but a meagre harvest, and this town, well inland on the mainland, was really the first place where the Gentile missionaries halted.

It was not till the second great journey, however, that St. Paul came down to Troas on the Asiatic coast of the Ægean, and gazed out over the island-strewn waters, towards Europe and towards the country which was the home of these two men—Macedonia. All along the way, as it seems to us, they had been prompting and suggesting that he should think of Europe as a field for his missionary zeal. But here in Troas, it would appear, one of the brothers plucked up courage and, in an interview with St. Paul, pleaded with all the passion of his pitiful heart that he would cross the sea and carry the Cross to his old home.

"And see," he would say, "our city stands on the great Roman highway which leads west and west through this mighty Empire towards the Adriatic, and towards Rome, the centre of the world. What an opportunity opens out before you there. Can you resist the call ? And we need you—oh, we need your message bitterly. There are men and women in this city of ours praying to God, lifting up hands blindly to the God they know not, longing for the light. I have seen them, little groups of them—a group of women especially, who, I think, must have some acquaintance with your own old Jewish faith, the faith that drew me first when I came to Asia—meeting for prayer in a quiet spot down by the banks of one of the streams, which flows close by the town. Will you not come ? Come ! Come over and help us ! "

And Paul listened, and his heart was stirred. He wondered, . . . but could not immediately make up his mind. And then in the night-time he had a dream. He saw again the man from Macedonia standing on that distant shore, which seemed to have drawn nearer in his dream, and on his face a look of wistful appeal, his hands outstretched in pleading. He saw the lips move, and he heard him say, " Come over into Macedonia and help us." We can see the friends meet next morning. " Have you made up your mind ? " asks the man from Macedonia. And Paul answers smilingly in the affirmative, " Yes, I am coming. I had a dream last night.

"A Man—A Certain Macedonian"

I saw you stand, and I heard you call. It is the leading of the Spirit of God. I am ready to answer and obey."

And so the momentous decision was made which has meant so much to Europe and to us to-day. For of all the personalities who have carved their names deepest on the soil of European history, St. Paul ranks higher than Napoleon or even the great Cæsar. The short voyage was made across Paul's Rubicon, from Troas to Nicopolis, and then the journey up country to Philippi. And on the day of the Jewish Sabbath the two brothers led the great missionary beyond the town and down by the banks of the stream. And there they found it even as they had said. A little band of women were praying. There were not many Jews in Philippi, and probably no synagogue. But, prompted by some irresistible desire they had been meeting there, praying humbly, yearningly that God would send some one to enlighten them. The scene starts vividly into view : these women engaged in earnest talk and prayer in this secluded place by the stream ; and the little band of men approaching, one of them stirred deeply by the sight. And there, by the stream, in the open air, the Cross was uplifted and magnified on European soil by the great missionary of the Gentiles. We can see these women intently listening. We can watch the growing excitement on their faces. We can hear them breaking out at length into exclamations of rapture and joy. And when Paul tells them the story of his dream in Troas, we can hear one of them exclaiming, " It is an answer—an answer to our prayers." And after Paul has finished his address, we can see the leader of that band of women introducing herself to Paul :

" I am not a native of Philippi. I am Lydia from Thyatira, in the land where you have been telling the great news. I am not a Jewess ; but I used to attend the synagogue in my native town, for I am a seeker after God, and of all the religions, that of the Jews drew me most ; for it seemed to be a worship of the one true God. But my heart was never fully satisfied. And now you come, out of the heart of that faith, bearing the very message that all men are yearning for here—concerning the Redeemer who died and rose again. Will you not stay with us for a while. I am able to lodge you. I am a trader in the purple cloths for which my city of Thyatira is famed, and I often have the merchants staying with me when they come with their bales. And many of those women whom you see here are employed by me. Stay, and tell your Good News to this needy town."

And Paul and his friends stayed. And soon the crowds began to draw in to Lydia's house to hear him. And in this house was probably formed the first Christian congregation on European soil. We recall the commotion the new religion made in the town. A woman who was something like a spiritualistic medium of our day—prompted by the men who made money by the messages which she professed to give from the other world, urged on, because this Paul was drawing away the poor, deluded people who were vainly seeking light in this direction—created a scene in the streets, a breach of the peace. And Paul and his fellow-missionary Silas were thrown into prison. And, as they sang praise to God among the criminals in the nighttime, the gaoler, who was also a seeker for Redemption, heard them ; and there was a commotion, and the doors were flung open; and the gaoler came trembling and cried, " What must I do to be saved ? "

It is a wonderfully exciting story, the story of the beginning of Paul's Gospel campaign in Europe. That spot by the river bank ought to be a sacred spot to us. And it ought to be a sacred house in Christian history, that house of Lydia the purple-seller from Thyatira. From this house, when he came back to it six or seven years later, Paul wrote one if not two of his letters to Corinth. And to this house—or to the church which began in this house—Paul wrote from his prison in Rome, some years later still, that beautiful letter to Philippi. It reads almost like a love-letter, so full is it of affection, and pride, and chivalry, and tender interest, and joy.

This aspect of the romantic story is too well known to call for details. But what about the mystery in which it began—the mystery of the two brothers through whose instrumentality the Cross was brought to Europe ?

We turn to the chapter in the book of Acts where the story is told (xvi). We see Paul wandering through Phrygia and Galatia, wondering if he should go next to the province of Asia; but the Spirit said " No." What does that mean ? How did the Spirit speak to him ? Was it not through human voices urging him to go elsewhere ? Then north through Mysia—nearer and nearer to the coast that faces Europe. Then he wonders if he should turn away east into Bithynia; but again the Spirit said " No." Was it not the dream of Europe already beginning to take hold of Paul ? Then further north he goes into the Troad, and down at last into the seaport of Troas. Then come the words

describing his dream.   Let us observe them closely.
" A man was (there), a certain Macedonian,
standing and beckoning him, and saying : ' Cross
into Macedonia : succour us.' "

" A man—a certain Macedonian." Vague certainly the words are, but not wholly indefinite, not
" a man who seemed from his appearance to be a
Macedonian " ; not just " a man, an unknown man,"
but " a certain particular man, a Macedonian."
Even if he had stood on the shore and gazed longingly
across the waters, he could hardly have seen the coast
of Macedonia. And in any case the longing was
there to be accounted for, before he had seen the
distant world of his dreams. Doubtless he had
seen the Macedonian dress on the streets of Troas,
but it was not so distinctive that only Macedonians
would wear it. No, it was the image of someone
Paul had met in waking life. Paul had recognised
the figure in his dream.   And the writer of the book
in using those words indicates that he knew him
too, and could name him if he cared. But he did
not choose to. Why ?

" Now when he had seen the vision, immediately
we endeavoured to set out for Macedonia, *mutually
confirming* each other (that is what the word translated " assuredly gathering " in our Bibles means)
that the Lord had called us to preach the Gospel
to them." " *We* endeavoured to make voyage—*we*."
The word occurs frequently in the book of Acts after
this ; but this is the first time it meets us unambigu-
ously. The writer of this book is now evidently
in the company of Paul. Where had he joined
him ? We turn back a few pages to the account
of Paul's first journey, and there we find that when
he was returning home he passed through Antioch,

the town on the borders between Pisidia and Phrygia,
and he confirmed the souls of the disciples, and
exhorted them to continue in the faith, " and that
we must through much tribulation enter into the
Kingdom of God." (Acts xiv. 22). This " we "
is not so clearly the sign-mark of the writer of the
book ; it might be just a bit of Paul's speech
reported directly. But surely it is only a hearer
who would so report the words. Was it here in
Pisidian Antioch that the writer, Luke, first met
Paul ? Let us go a little further back to the
account of Paul's first visit to this city (Acts xiii.
14-52). It is the fullest account of Paul's doings
in any of the cities of this journey, and the language
is very circumstantial. The writer describes Paul
going to the synagogue on the Sabbath and sitting
among the audience (xii. 14). We see the rulers
sending down the synagogue to where they were
sitting, with a message for the strangers (xiii. 15).
And we see Paul standing up, contrary to the usual
Jewish mode, and beckoning with his hand—a
frequently recorded gesture of his—before he began
to speak (xiii. 16). The details of the address are
full, and many of them are fresh. We are told
of the seven nations whom God destroyed in Canaan
(xiii. 19), that the period of the judges was 450
years (xiii. 20), and that King Saul reigned forty
years over Israel, a fact nowhere recorded in the
Old Testament (xiii. 21). But, more important
still, many of the phrases have the authentic Pauline
ring about them—" repentance," " salvation,"
" glad tidings," " the promise fulfilled." He tells also
of God raising Jesus from the dead, and that " He
was seen many days." And finally comes this typically
Pauline verse : " Through this Man is preached

unto you the forgiveness of sins, and by Him all that believe are justified from all things from which ye could not be justified by the Law of Moses" (38). This is no address composed by the writer and put into the lips of Paul. It is obviously compiled from actual recollections of what the Apostle said.

But there is one carefully noted feature of the address which seems to bring us into contact with the reporter himself. We are told that Paul addressed not merely the " men of Israel," but the " God-fearers " (xiii. 16, 26)—the seeking souls among the pagans who had become adherents of the synagogue. And we are informed that Paul said, " to them also was this word of salvation sent." Further, that it was the Gentiles who besought him to stay and speak to them again (xiii. 42). And that when the congregation was broken up, it was not only Jews but many of the " God-fearers " who followed Paul. And we are told of the joy of the Gentiles when Paul finally turned to them. " They were glad and glorified the word of the LORD ; and as many as were ordained to eternal life believed " (xiii. 46, 48). Is not the writer among those rejoicing ones ? Is not he among those who believed ? Does not that word " as many as were ordained to eternal life " reflect the feelings of this pagan whom the hound of heaven had tracked out in this barbarous land ? Like every soul profoundly moved at the time of God's finding of him, he is convinced that it was part of the eternal Purpose of God for him. May it not be to this town Eusebius refers when he says that " in respect of race, Luke was one of the group of Antiocheans." It was here he was won, though all his subsequent Christian activity lay in other fields.

"A Man—A Certain Macedonian"

One other circumstance makes this reading of the story extremely probable. When Paul first reached Antioch he was wretchedly ill, as he tells us himself (Gal. iv. 13-15), so ill that outside aid had to be called in. Surely it is this chance, which was no chance but the providential ordering of God for him, that Luke refers to when he speaks of being ordained to eternal life ? *He* was the medical man who was called in to treat the great Apostle, and in his contact with him was strangely stirred by the man's faith. Truly this sickness of Paul's turned out to the glory of God. And if Luke and his brother were won in Antioch of Pisidia, it would be from this point that they became companions of Paul, when he returned on his second great journey which led eventually to Europe. Were *they* not the men through whom the Spirit spoke, when Paul was guided by the evident hand of God to Troas ?

Back to that point our story has carried us once more. The dream had shown Paul " a man, a certain Macedonian " ; and thereafter Luke slips himself in unobtrusively as a member of the party. Let us follow the record of the narrative. " Setting out then from Troas, we ran a straight course to Samothrace, and on the next day to Neapolis, and thence to Philippi." The swift course of the narrative convinces us that this was their predetermined journey's end for the meantime. Why Philippi ? Let the historian himself give his own reason. ". . . Philippi," he calls the place, " which is the first city of the province of Macedonia, a (Roman) *colonia*." Now there is no other town in all his writings that the writer troubles to tell us so much about. Later, he displays an astonishing accuracy as to the titles by which the Roman guardians of the law styled themselves in this town. And it is not as if he were writing long after the glory of Philippi had passed. He was writing for his own day of a city which every one knew of without any advertisement on his part. Why does he trouble to tell all this about Philippi ? " The first city of the district," he calls it, and in that very word the reason begins to be apparent. For we know from other sources, that it was not regarded by everybody as the first town of the district. There was quite a rivalry between Thessalonica, Amphipolis, and Philippi for the pre-eminence. Each was a little jealous of the other. The writer in fact is clearly taking a side in the matter here. He is a partisan. But who would trouble to show his predilection in an unessential matter of this kind— except a citizen, jealous for his city's status ? The modest Luke, in short, here gives himself away. *He* was a native of Philippi—he was a *Macedonian*.

And why does he trouble to tell us it was a Roman colony ? There are three or four other towns mentioned in the Acts which shared the same dignity—Corinth, Lystra, Ptolemais, yes, even Antioch in Pisidia. Yet this is the only one that Luke is careful to remind us about. He was proud of the special privilege of his native city. Luke further betrays himself. Does it not seem as if he himself belonged to a family of Roman origin ? The only region indeed in which we find a name like " Lukas " indigenous is the South of Italy ; " Lukas " being the shortened Greek form of " Lucanus."

But we are still not at the end of our discoveries. " And on the Sabbath day we went out of the city by a river side, where it was thought there was a place of prayer," the historian goes on. "It was thought." Who thought it? One MS. reads "*we* thought." Evidently Paul was led out there by these Macedonian friends. Luke had observed this meeting for prayer in by-gone days. Nor is this proof of local familiarity the only one. For when he tells of Paul and Silas being led before the magistrate, he adds in a kind of parenthesis, that the city magistrates were known as the *strategoi*, that is to say in Latin terms, the praetors, the military town-majors appointed there by Rome. And archæological investigation has proved his minute accuracy in this as in other details of the life of the town. It all goes to corroborate the view that he was a native of the place.

But still the full tale is not told. The next chapter of his book begins: "Now when *they* had passed through Amphipolis and Apollonia *they* came to Thessalonica." And the sentence betrays the fact that the writer of the book was left behind in Philippi when Paul passed on to visit the other cities of Greece. And we have to turn over a good many pages of the history before we find Luke saying "we" again. Instead of crossing direct from Attica to Asia, Paul had to come back through Macedonia to escape from the toils of malevolent Jews who had intended to make away with him on the voyage. He passed through Philippi; and the writer then carries on the narrative as a companion: "*We* sailed away from Philippi." This was some five to seven years after Paul's first arrival in the town. So Luke, having won his heart's desire, stayed all that time to confirm the work of Paul in his native city.

Without penetrating further into the evidence afforded by the writer's own narrative, we turn elsewhere to pick up another line of evidence. But we must note first the touching fact that from this time on (56 A.D.) Luke practically never, except for one short interval, leaves his hero's side. He accompanies him to Jerusalem, keeps watch over his interests during his arrest and imprisonment; follows him to Cæsarea, when he is removed there for greater safety; sails with him to Rome; and is his constant companion during nearly all the time of his imprisonment there. The one interval of absence was apparently shortly after their arrival in Rome. For when Paul writes his letter to Philippi, Luke is not mentioned at the end. But when he writes a little later to Colossæ, and to his friend Philemon, Luke's greetings are sent as well as his own. Where had Luke gone? Polycarp seems to be aware of more than one letter to Philippi (*Polyc. Phil. III.*). Is it not likely that Luke conveyed one? When Aristarchus and he left Paul, Aristarchus would have gone to Thessalonica, his native town. It is natural to suppose that Luke went to his. Moreover, Paul had heard of the doings of the Church in Philippi before he wrote. Epaphroditus brought him word. Is it not likely that Luke would have sent a letter by his hands? He came bearing a money gift, which the Philippian Church had sent in concern for his needs. Who would have told them of Paul's needs unless one of the two who had accompanied him to Rome? Then is there no hint in the letter to Philippi of Luke's being amongst them? Whom does Paul call his " true yokefellow "? Luther suggested that it must be the chief presbyter. Certainly he would

be the one to receive the letter first. But Luke
had been the chief presbyter when the Church was
founded, and for a few years thereafter. If he
had returned to Philippi would he not just resume
his old place ? And to whom would Paul appeal
to heal the strife, if not to one who had not been a
party to the dissension ? The probabilities all
point to Luke having returned to Philippi. And
again the view that Luke belonged to the place is
confirmed (Phil. iv. 3).

But to build on an argument from silence would
be flimsy building if that were all, and so we
turn to pursue the other lines of evidence.

Thrice only is Luke named in the New Testament,
and never by himself, only by Paul. The latest
is probably that reference in the end of the
second epistle to Timothy (2 Tim. iv. 11) where
we have certainly a bit of a genuine letter of
Paul's. He is bidding Timothy come to see
him as soon as he can, for all his friends have
left him. " Only Luke is with me." It is a beautiful
testimony—all the sweeter because it is bare statement of fact—to the character of the man, his
constancy, his devotion, his self-effacing loyalty to
his hero and friend. Paul's other references to Luke
by name are in the letter to Colossæ, and the private
letter written at the same time to Philemon, one of
the leading Christians of that Church in Colossæ.
" Lucas sends greetings to thee," he writes to
Philemon, and in the letter to Colossæ he writes :
" the doctor Lucas, the (my) well-beloved, greets
you." It may only be because Luke was present
with him that he adds his greeting, though Luke
may have been acquainted with the Church and
with Philemon. But it is a noble description to

have earned from the great Apostle's lips. It gives us a tender glimpse of the man's kindly and compassionate heart (Philem. 24 ; Col. iv. 14).

But this word "doctor" forms the starting-point for our next line of evidence. It is the ground of the conjecture that it was Luke who had been called in, when the Apostle fell ill in Pisidian Antioch. In which case there doubtless mingles the memory of Luke's devoted attentions, in that word which Paul wrote to the Galatians : "I bear you record, that, if it had been possible, you would have plucked out your own eyes, and have given them to me" (Gal. iv. 15).

Luke was more than a mere professional medical man. He has become such out of sheer love of the calling. The blessed ministry of healing had appealed to the man's noble and pitiful heart. We spoke of the cult of Asklēpios, when we began this story, a cult which was well known in the regions of Macedonia and Thessaly—the worship, namely, of the god who was Healer and Saviour. We fancied it must have appealed to this man in his pagan days. Surely we can find an echo of it in the New Testament phrase which, there is reason for believing, is used by Luke alone, "God the Saviour," or "our Saviour God" ; and is applied even to Christ. In the *Magnificat*, Mary says "My spirit has rejoiced in God my Saviour" (Luke i. 47). And in the pastoral epistles where the phrase recurs, it seems always to be in quotations from a manual, "The Discipline of our Saviour God" (Tit. ii. 10), which was probably written by Luke, as a linguistic examination suggests (1 Tim. iv. 10; Tit. ii. 10, 13, iii. 4).

In this title "doctor," we begin to see reason for believing Luke to be, not a Jew but a Greek, or a

Greco-Roman. For medicine was a profession practised almost exclusively by the Greeks in those days. It is not impossible indeed that Luke had visited the schools of Tarsus, for medicine was studied there. At any rate the *Materia Medica* of Dioscorides, who had studied at Tarsus, and was a perhaps younger contemporary of Luke, seems to have been read by Luke. The preface to his Gospel has every appearance of being modelled on the preface to Dioscorides' book. The medical language employed by Luke has been abundantly demonstrated in recent years. But we have only to think of his Gospel, and of the special interest he shows in all the cures effected by Jesus, to realise that this was one feature of the Saviour's work on earth which drew him with a special tenderness. His Saviour was indeed the Healer, the Divine Physician of the bodies as well as the souls of men.

There is clear evidence too in Luke's writings not only of his medical training, but of his general Greek culture as well. There is no finer or more literary Greek in all the New Testament. He seems indeed to have been somewhat of a poet, for probably those Hymns in the beginning of his Gospel—the *Benedictus*, the *Magnificat*, the *Nunc Dimittis*, as well as other quoted fragments from his manual of Discipline (1 Tim. iii. 16; 2 Tim. ii. 11f.) are compositions of his. Renan thinks that the Gospel, not only in its literary style, but in the special emphasis it lays on Christ's vocation to the poor, the suffering, the outcasts, the aliens from society, is the most beautiful book in the world.

This evidence that he was a Greek would, of itself alone, be inconclusive. But it is clinched by Paul's reference to Luke in the letter to Colossæ.

When Paul sends greetings (iv. 10), he adds at the end of the first group of names, "men of the circumcision." It is only after he has done so that Luke is mentioned. He was a Gentile; and in the reverence for Jewish Law and usage, which can be seen in his writings, we seem to see proof that he was one of the Greek-speaking pagan adherents of the synagogue—"the God-fearers."

We now reach the last stage of the evidence which clears up the mystery of the two brothers, with which our story began. Paul's third, or as it is sometimes called, his intermediate letter to the Corinthians, has this interesting piece of information to give us: "I enlisted Titus and deputed *a* brother (our Bible translation says) to accompany him." Literally it is "*the* brother"; and the phrase can mean nothing else than "*his* brother" (2 Cor. xii. 18).

And then, ill at ease till he heard the result of this agitated mission to the recalcitrant Church, he went to Macedonia to meet the returning deputies half-way. The news when it came was reassuring, and he wrote, apparently from Philippi, a fourth letter, in which these interesting references occur. Just one thing remained to be done—the making of the collection in Corinth for the poor Christians in Jerusalem. And he intimates to the Corinthians that he is sending Titus to help in that. "And we are sending along with him the brother, whose praise in the Gospel is in all the churches, and who moreover has been elected by the churches as our fellow-traveller in connection with this grace which is being ministered by us." Why does Paul not mention the name of this brother? Is it that in his courtesy he is respecting the modesty of the man to whom he is referring ? And then that phrase " the brother "—it has lost its real significance for us, through our habit of taking it as a term of Christian fellowship. It is often used thus no doubt. But the words here almost certainly mean, as in the previous letter, " *his* brother," the brother, namely, of Titus. " His praise in the Gospel," Paul refers to. The phrase does not justify us in saying—with some—that this man was famous among the churches because he had written a Gospel. But does it not mean that the man's knowledge of the Gospel story was beginning to be acknowledged all over the churches, at least in Greece and Macedonia ? Here is a man who is already beginning to collect all the details of the great story of redeeming Love that he can lay his hands on ; and he has made it his task to go round the Greek churches, teaching them the great facts of the Divine Life, into fellowship with which they had been called. We can at least say this, that if this man had any skill with the pen at all, and if he ever had the leisure to do so, it would be his plain duty to write down the amazing story in some form which would become the permanent possession of the churches (2 Cor. viii. 18).

So, when later on in the same letter (ix. 3) Paul writes : " I am sending the brothers," and again (ix. 5) : " I have thought it necessary to urge the brothers that they would go before unto you," he is referring to the men as brothers by blood. There is a note at the end of our second letter to Corinth which says " written from Philippi of Macedonia by Titus and Lucas." Whether it refers to the third or fourth letter to Corinth matters not. The note is significant and its authority is not lightly to be set aside. When we turn back to Luke's history of this time, we find words which corroborate our identification of this modest " brother," who does not like his name mentioned, as Luke. After the letters, Paul went himself by-and-by to Corinth. That he was unaccompanied by Luke is apparent from the historian's language : " When *he* had gone over those parts (that is, Macedonia) . . . *he* came to Greece." But that Luke accompanied him *from* Corinth again, when he set out on his journey overland to Jerusalem, is equally apparent from what follows. After mentioning that the other friends had been sent by sea Luke writes : " They went on and waited for *us* at Troas." The natural inference is that Luke had been sent to Corinth, before the Apostle had proceeded thither.

When we remember all that we now know of the character of the man who wrote the third Gospel and the Acts, one other remarkable fact which we here add, seems to confirm our reading of the story. Luke, who never mentions his own name in the Acts, never once mentions the name of Titus either. Surely the only satisfactory explanation is that Titus was his brother by blood, and that Luke is equally reticent, equally unwilling to thrust even his brother's name into the great story. And yet Titus had played a great and worthy part in the drama. He was among the first Gentile leaders of the Church ; was known in Galatia (Gal. ii. 1) ; a familiar figure in Corinth (2 Cor. ii. 13, vii. 5-7, viii. 6. 16-19) ; and he, too, was among Paul's earliest converts (Gal. ii. 1, 3 ; Tit. i. 4).

These then were the two brothers who hailed originally from Philippi. And Luke is the modest Macedonian to whose pleading we owe the fact that

"A Man—A Certain Macedonian"

Paul was induced to cross to European soil, and plant the Cross amid the old spent gods of Greek paganism. To the end of the chapter Luke went on effacing himself. He never married, tradition tells us. He gladly and willingly gave up all public honour in the Church to become the guardian and medical attendant of the old, worn, and physically enfeebled Apostle Paul. His heart seems to have been broken when Paul met his martyr death. It seems likely from the way the book of Acts ends that he meant to write a third volume carrying the story further. But it was never accomplished. Perhaps he never could bring himself to set down the tragedy in cold black and white.

Still, in the leisure time which this devotion of his life to the offices of friendship gave him, he has enriched the world, he has made the Church to all time immeasurably his debtor, by writing the history of these great days of the beginning ; and, above all, by writing the sweet and winsome Gospel which bears his name. It contains much that the world would have been infinitely the poorer to have missed. It alone contains the story of the Prodigal Son. Benighted Europe was " the far country " for Luke; and he induced the missionary to the Gentiles to come, bringing the story of the Good Shepherd to that continent.

CHAPTER VII

"Eye-Witnesses from the Beginning," and "Certain Others"

I

THERE is in each of us a little wholesome scepticism. It is the grain of salt which we apply to every exceptional story we hear. We fancy it is too wonderful to be credible, too good to be true. We say to the teller of it, Who told you? This wondering doubt does not by any means desert us when we are confronted with the Gospel story. We may by-and-by reach the conviction that it is too good to be false; but it is such an amazing story, the "news" it brings is so "good," that the mind in its more secular moods wonders if it can be fact. And of the evangelists also we fain would ask, Who told you? Are you sure that your witnesses can be trusted?

It is not enough to be told that they are the treasures of the well-kept storehouse of early Church tradition, though that is in large measure true. We want to see that tradition precipitating itself in the minds of well-known and credible witnesses. In the case of the first two Gospels this desire can to a large extent be satisfied. The earliest Gospel was written by John Mark. Mark was a son of the house of the Upper Room. Jesus was a friend of the family, in the later days of His ministry. Peter was practically an inmate of this house in the weeks that followed Calvary. Peter was the means of winning Mark for Christ (1 Peter v. 13), probably in these weeks. According to a trustworthy tradition which Eusebius quotes from Papias, Mark in later years became Peter's amanuensis and interpreter; and his Gospel is a collection of Peter's reminiscences of his Lord. The weight of Peter's authority lies behind this record, and it is sufficient to satisfy all but the most fastidious minds.

When we turn to the Gospel according to Matthew, two facts at once become apparent. One is that, for the larger part of the narrative, this Gospel is dependent upon Mark's, has indeed engrossed almost all of it, often simply transcribing Mark's words. The second fact is, that the greater part of what remains in Matthew consists of sayings of Jesus—four or five large groups of them, as well as isolated words. When we compare these laws, parables, revelations, denunciations, with similar passages in Luke's Gospel, we learn that both have, for these, relied on a single source, a source which has come to be called the Logia, and which, there is good reason to believe, was compiled by the disciple Matthew. Satisfied about these two authentic witnesses, we do not feel so anxious to enquire who was the editor who joined the two documents together, in this Gospel which bears the name of the second of them. But there are some stories which are peculiar to Matthew's Gospel alone. The carpenter's hesitation to marry Mary, the coming of the Wise Men from the East, the flight to Egypt, the massacre of the Innocents, the return to Nazareth, and John the Baptiser's reluctance to baptise Jesus, form one group in the early part of the narrative. Peter's attempt to walk on the water, his receiving the power of the keys, his catching of the fish to pay the Temple tax, form another group in the centre of the Gospel. And in Jerusalem during Passion week, there are the stories of the city's commotion when Jesus rode in on the ass, of the children shouting and singing in the Temple courts next day, of Jesus' question to Judas when he greeted Him in the garden, of Judas and the blood-money, of Pilate's wife's dream, of Pilate's basin, of the resurrection of saints at the crucifixion, of the sealing of the tomb, and of the bribing of the guard. Where did the editor get these three groups of stories—birth stories, "Peter" stories, Passion stories ? It is noticeable that each group contains one or more wonder-stories—Joseph's dreams, the star-guided wise men, Peter on the water, Peter and the fish, Pilate's wife's dream, the resurrection of saints. The Passion stories, particularly the last two, suggest that they were current in the early Church in Jerusalem. The "Peter" stories are probably from the same source, and they reflect the prominence of that disciple there in the early days. But the legendary touch about them suggests that they had grown up some time after he was gone from the city. The birth stories, again, gather round the father of the Holy Family, and we are strongly reminded that the second son of the family, James, was also a prominent figure in the early Jerusalem Church. The House of Alphai—the relatives of Matthew, who wrote the diary of the Sayings—held an important place in the Church which gathered round James in Jerusalem. And it is probable that the compilation which we have in the Gospel according to Matthew was effected in Jerusalem or among the Judæan Christians. But it is impossible to determine more precisely to whom these stories are due. Nor does it greatly matter. To feel with a measure of confidence that we have the authority of Peter and Matthew behind the important sections of this Gospel's testimony is to be satisfied here too.

It is with the writings of Luke that we are now to be concerned. He wrote the great history of the early days, *The Acts of the Apostles ;* he is the author of the *Third Gospel.* He himself was an eyewitness of a considerable part of the events in the closing chapters of *Acts.* But for a large part he had to depend on other informants ; and of no part of his Gospel story does he claim to give authentic first-hand testimony. He does claim, however, to have got his information from properly accredited witnesses. Who were they ?

We ask this question with special interest about his Gospel, because some of the most appealing incidents and parables belonging to the Immortal Story are to be found in the pages of Luke alone. What an impoverishment of our sacred literature it would have meant to be without the parables of the Good Samaritan, the Lazy Neighbour, The Wily Steward, the Unjust Judge, the Rich Man and Lazarus, the Pharisee and the Publican, the Lost Coin, and the Prodigal Son. And when we recall the stories of the shepherds, the Twelve-year old in the Temple, the widow of Nain, the sinner-woman who anointed Jesus' feet in Galilee, the peril of Jesus from Herod's designs, Zacchæus, Martha and Mary, the dying thief, the two on the road to Emmaus— it is of Luke we feel inclined to ask this question most of all, Who told you ? He, too, had a copy of Mark's Gospel and Matthew's diary before him. Where did he get these documents ? Who told him the stories which he alone retails ?

If we accompany him on his travels after he had become a follower of Christ, we may learn—in part at least. Like his fellow-practitioner in Browning's story, he, too, was " a picker-up of learning's crumbs." That he had set himself to glean details and to make memoranda of all he heard, his writings themselves betray. For nearly half the course of his history of the Apostolic days, our attention is arrested by his frequent use of the word " we." He is reminding us that he himself was an eye-witness. Indeed, from this personal note, and from the extraordinary vividness of the narrative, in which we can still catch the glow and excitement of the events, as though his heart beat fast while he wrote, we feel that he is making a practically verbatim copy from the notes of his journal. Harnack says : " They have about them the character of a diary." May we not infer that besides his notes of events he actually experienced, he made notes of other people's stories ?

When friends meet, the first events of the past they recall are the immediate ones. As the interview prolongs itself, they dip back further and further into the past. As Luke met with this one and the next, he would listen first to their connection with the happenings of Apostolic days, and then, by-and-by, if these friends happened to have been followers of Jesus, he would listen to their reminiscences of those celestial nights and days. We will follow the same order, only instead of mingling a strand of Apostolic history with a strand of Gospel story in alternate order, we will listen to the Apostolic history as we company with Luke, and then retrace the road and listen to the fragments of the Gospel story that some of these friends had to tell.

II

Paul was ill when he first reached Antioch of Pisidia, and a medical man was called in. It was the supreme moment in Dr. Luke's career. The tender-hearted physician was deeply impressed by the burning, dauntless spirit of the little Jew, and in the synagogue which this Gentile proselyte attended, he heard him tell on Sabbath his exciting tale of the advent of Him whom that race had long expected. It satisfied Luke's restless spirit, and he was won. He gave thanks to God that he had been " ordained to eternal life." (Acts xiii. 48). Yet only when Paul came to Antioch on his second journey did Luke join him as a companion. But from this point onward, he would be tireless in his questioning of all who came his way, as to how the Divine story began. Clearly he was in contact all the time with witnesses of the Apostolic deeds, and we need do little more than record the names. There may be doubt concerning the portions of the story each was responsible for, but there can be none about the men themselves. Naturally Paul would tell him of the ecstatic moment on the road to Damascus, when the holy light of the eternal Truth first dawned and shone about him brighter than the noon-day sun. Then he would tell how, in the city, Ananias the disciple had given him his commission. There, amid growing hostility, he bore his earliest testimony to Christ. After a time he went up to the Holy City, and was introduced to some of the disciples.

Courageously he bore his testimony on the scene of his persecuting zeal. Again his life was in danger, so he left the city; and for eleven years he was lost to the Church in the seclusion of Tarsus (ix. 1-31).

When Luke questioned him about the days of his persecuting activities, he was silent, and begged Silas, his associate on this journey, to proceed. From Silas Luke would learn the story of the first Christian martyr, who by his advocacy loosed the Truth of Christ from the trammels of ancient Judaism, testifying finally with his blood. Painfully he would tell of the part Paul had played in that deed of blood (vi. 1-viii. 3).

Then comes Paul's story, which we have already had before us. Those who were scattered abroad in that time of persecution had come to Antioch in Syria, and proclaimed the message there with much success. Barnabas was sent down from Jerusalem to visit the new community of Christians, and stayed on to encourage them. By-and-by he came all the way to Tarsus to entice Paul to join them in the work. It was the opportunity for which he (Paul) had been longing, and he greedily snatched it, dedicating himself to a life-long atonement for his crime. The first important piece of work in which he was associated with Barnabas was the conveying of famine-relief to the brethren in Judæa. In Jerusalem he had stayed with Barnabas' relatives, the family of John Mark. From them he heard the excited story of the slaying of James of Zabdai, of the imprisonment of Peter, and of his amazing escape, when he appeared in the dead of night at the door, and startled those who were gathered there in anxious prayer.

Barnabas and he returned to Antioch, when their

errand was completed, taking John Mark with them. Soon they were sent out on their first campaign. Mark accompanied. As the terrors of the journey loomed more and more menacing ahead, Mark's spirit failed him and he fled. We have already listened to the tale thus far (xi. 19-xiii. 13). But it is Luke himself who tells how Barnabas and Paul had come to Pisidian Antioch alone. Well he might remember their coming. It was the birthday of his soul.

It was not till he was on the way up to Jerusalem with Paul on his last visit to the city that Luke began to hear fragments of the still earlier Apostolic story. When they landed at Cæsarea they stayed some nights in the house of Philip the evangelist, one of the famous Seven, and once more the questioning began. The tragic ending of his friend Stephen's career had been the beginning of days for Philip too. A marked man because of his association with Stephen, he had fled from the capital to Samaria, and in that city preached the word with power. So great was his success that Peter and John came down from Jerusalem to see the work. But as usual trouble arose, and he travelled south towards Gaza in the desert, encountering the Ethiopian eunuch on the way. Afterwards he preached among the cities of the Shephelah (viii. 4-40).

When Paul's company set out from Cæsarea, they came, apparently, at the end of the first day's journey to Lydda, where the old disciple Mnason entertained them. The Cross had had its triumphs in that place. There was Peter's visit to the town to tell about ; his subsequent experiences in Joppa ; and something also of his experiences among the Gentiles in Cæsarea (ix. 32-xi. 18). But Luke was to hear more of this directly.

Reaching Jerusalem with Paul, he joined at length the company of some of the first disciples and followers of Jesus, and here the earliest chapter of the Church's story would be told. Peter and John are associated together in one of the stories; from their lips he doubtless heard it. Going up together to the Temple one day they had healed a lame man at the gate. A crowd collected, and Peter preached to them in Solomon's porch. Five thousand souls were won. The two disciples were arrested and at their trial next day, when they were enjoined not to preach any more in this Name, they answered, "Whether it be right in the sight of God to hearken unto you more than unto God, judge ye." They were dismissed, and returned to the Upper Room, where, in response to the ecstatic prayers of the company, the Holy Spirit fell. A great time followed. Rich believers shared their possessions with the poor. There was the solemn fate of Ananias and Sapphira to recall, and the growing power of Peter and the apostles with the crowd, as in Solomon's porch they continued to witness to Christ (iii. 1-v. 16).

A story lies embedded in this narrative, which is thought by some to be another version of the same facts. It was evidently given to Luke by someone who remembered first and chiefly the spiritual excitement of the Upper Room, the descent of the Spirit at Pentecost. It tells of the phenomenon of tongues, of Peter's sermon in the open, and of the winning of three thousand souls. It also tells of the community of possessions, of the imprisonment of the apostles, of the arraignment, of Peter's retort "We must obey God rather than men," of Gamaliel's counsel, of the dismissal of the Apostles and the continuance of their propaganda (ii. 1-47, v. 17-42).

"Eye-Witnesses from the Beginning"

It was told to Luke, perhaps by John Mark or some other frequenter of the Upper Room, someone with a more naïve and less orderly mind. And others of the disciple-circle would carry their reminiscences back behind these days, and tell of the long waiting in the Upper Room, in the interval between Calvary and Pentecost (i). Peter must have repeated the account of his visit to the sea-board lands, and his experience in Cornelius the centurion's house in Cæsarea.

But Luke had but brief time in which to pursue his investigations. The storm, which had long been brewing against Paul, broke out fiercely before they were many days in Jerusalem. And ere they could realise what had happened, Paul's long imprisonment had begun. Luke accompanied him to Cæsarea by-and-by. He had got together most of his notes for the earlier part of the history; and we can see him beguiling the tedium of the sad years, while he waited near his friend, and between the interruptions of journeys to Antioch to interview Paul's old friends for him, by arranging the material of these notes in a first tentative draft of a narrative of the great moving of the Spirit in the hearts of men.

And the first thing he would do would be to compare and adjust them with the notes of the diary he had kept during all the time he had companied with Paul on his last adventurous journeys which had ended in this imprisonment at length. Let us look over his shoulder while he glances through the notes of this second part of the story. The first entry is his own story. It is his account of the visit of Paul and Barnabas to the town of Antioch in Pisidia. There is a very full note of the sermon

Paul preached, and of the result for him and many others (xiii. 14-52).

He had never got a very full account of the rest of that journey of Barnabas and Paul. But now that he was in touch with Antioch, Paul seemed to be anxious to see Barnabas again. And Luke would be the go-between. Between the two, the whole journey and the events that followed would be cleared up at last. He himself could add a note about Paul's passing through Antioch on his return journey (xiv. 1-28).

After this journey, the trouble about the Gentile converts became acute, and the story of the great Council in Jerusalem, as we have it in Luke's history, was possibly told him by Barnabas, for Paul's own account is not quite so conciliatory (Gal. ii.). No doubt he had heard a good deal about it before he left the Holy City, something at least of the speeches which Peter, and James, the brother of the Lord, had made in support of Paul's main contention; and he may have got a sight of the letter containing the decrees (xv. 1-33).

Luke would next hunt out the notes he had of the second great mission-journey of the Apostle. It was Silas, Paul's associate on this journey, who had given him these, and now that he had seen Paul and Barnabas reconciled, and had heard something of the dispute from their own lips, he would be able to put the tale in order. Paul and Silas journeyed over the old ground first, delivering the decrees. It was on this journey that Paul took young Timothy into his company (xv. 35-xvi. 5).

Then once more Luke is an eye-witness. It is the story of how Paul was induced to come to Europe, but Luke had modestly suppressed the part he himself played in the transaction—soliciting so earnestly all along the road from Antioch, that Paul felt the Spirit closing door after door against his inclinations—the road to Asia, and the road to Bithynia, until at last he is in Troas, and the debate is settled by a dream. Philippi becomes the scene of his first planting of the Cross in Europe (xvi. 6-24). The story of what happened in the Philippian prison to Paul and Silas was probably told to Luke by Silas (xvi. 25-40).

During the next part of Paul's activities he was a good deal alone. Luke himself had stayed behind in his native Philippi, and did not rejoin him for five or six years. To Paul therefore he must have been indebted for the reminiscences that follow—Paul's journey from Philippi through Macedonia to Achaia, his experiences in Thessalonica and Berœa, his disappointing visit to Athens, where his attempt to approach them along the line of philosophy resulted mainly in ridicule and failure. He left for Corinth, resolving all along the road not to know anything among them save Jesus Christ and Him crucified. Then follows the romantic story of his meeting with Priscilla and Aquila. Certain turns of phrase strongly suggest that Paul was the teller. Luke seems for example to have put down on his note-book once a fragment of the direct speech of Paul when he " reasoned with them out of the scriptures opening and alleging that Christ must needs have suffered and risen again from the dead ; and that *this Jesus whom I preach unto you,* is Christ." Clearly it was from Paul that the story of his sojourn in Athens came. For Paul was alone in Athens, and the phrase " his spirit was stirred within him," could only have come from Paul.

Here again we read that he "disputed in the synagogue," and a similar phrase occurs in the account of his doings at Corinth, "he reasoned in the synagogue." The expression "Paul was pressed in spirit," and again the direct speech in the following verse, and the account of his dream in Corinth, all bear out the impression that Paul himself was the narrator (xvii. 1-xviii. 11). Timothy and Silas had rejoined him at this point, and possibly they recounted the episode before the Roman Gallio (xviii. 12-17).

Then Paul parted from the brethren once more, and crossed to Ephesus with his new friends Priscilla and Aquila. Partly from Paul himself, partly from these two, when Luke met them either on the way up to Jerusalem or a few years later, he may have got some of the details of the Apostle's experiences in Ephesus. Paul did not stay long there at this time, and certainly the story which follows, of the appearance of Apollos in Ephesus, and of the half-formed Christians whom he left behind—scarcely more than followers of the Baptist—seems almost certainly to have come from Priscilla and Aquila (xviii. 24-xix. 7). But the account of Paul's brief visit (xviii. 18-23), and the long story of his subsequent visit to Ephesus, come apparently from the Apostle himself. The personal note (xviii. 21, xix. 21), and the statement about Paul's own desire to speak to the mob in the theatre (xix. 30), betray the teller. It is Paul's account of what he afterwards described as "fighting with wild beasts at Ephesus" (xix. 8-41).

The rest of the book of the Acts is practically all from the diary of Luke, who shortly after the Ephesian visit was the constant companion of the Apostle. It is the story of the ascent to Jerusalem, of the

uproar in that city, of the imprisonment of the
Apostle, of his appeal to Cæsar, of the long and
exciting voyage and tempest and shipwreck—
vividly related—and of his reception in Rome
(xx-xxviii). Particulars here and there throughout
the whole book may have been added by various
individuals—such as Gaius and Aristarchus of
Macedonia, and Epaphras of Colossæ, and Titus,
who was probably Luke's own brother, and Nicolas
the proselyte of Antioch, and other leaders of that
city's church.

Whether we are right in all the allocations of the
various parts of the narrative to these different
eye-witnesses or not, we need have no hesitation
in accepting Luke's claim that his narrative was
received from eye-witnesses,—and these the men
here named.

III

It is for his Gospel that Luke makes his express
claim to have sought out eye-witnesses. And it is
about the Gospel that we most eagerly ask who
these were. Who were the men and women with
whom he had had opportunity of associating on his
Gospel-journeyings, who could tell him about the
events in Jesus' lifetime ? Let us retraverse the
journey in his company once again.

For the critical discussion on which the views
here put forward are based, the writer may be permitted to refer to certain articles on *The Passion
Journey of Jesus*, which appeared in the *Expositor*
(January to May, 1919). We would tell the tale
quite simply here. Nearly all that is peculiar to

Luke's Gospel is found in this section of his Gospel (ix. 51-xviii. 14). There are a number of details in the Passion Story as Luke records it. There are also the birth narratives, some of the details of the Baptiser's addresses to the people, some information about the Nazareth address, the story about the draught of fish at the time of the calling of the fishermen disciples, the parable about the preference of old wine to new, the raising of the widow of Nain's son, and the story of the anointing in Galilee. All these latter, with a few other details, are in the earlier chapters. It is for this body of special information that we have to find eye-witnesses.

When Luke joined Paul, on his last missionary journey, at Pisidian Antioch, it was Silas who was Paul's chief associate. Silas was one of the deputation of two which had been sent down to the Gentile Churches with the decision of the Jerusalem Council. He was the broader-minded of the two ; his mind was of the fervently spiritual, not the coldly legal type ; prophetic, not preceptual. He favoured, we may assume, Paul's point of view. The second century ecstatics, known as the Montanists, claim him as their spiritual ancestor. His prophetic and evangelistic gift must have appealed to Paul. And when Paul broke fellowship with Barnabas—and it was not merely a quarrel over the unfortunate Mark ; it was a difference of outlook as well (Gal. ii. 13)—he invited Silas to join him. That fact is in itself a testimony to the religious outlook of Silas. He was no doubt a powerful and moving speaker ; and Luke may have listened with particular attention when he spoke. What would specially awaken Luke's interest was the fact that in Silas' addresses he would often hear him say : " I heard the Lord speak these words." For Silas, who was reckoned a " chief man among the brethren," must have been so for the usual reason in the Jerusalem Church : he belonged to the believers of the beginning, he had been a follower of the Lord. Tradition, with some appearance of probability, makes him one of the Seventy. For he seems entitled to the designation " Apostle" (1 Thess. ii. 6)—one of those who had " seen the Lord."

It seems to us that somewhere on this missionary journey Luke heard Silas give a powerful address on the last things, and that he made notes of it. It consisted largely of words that Jesus had said to His disciples on the way up to Jerusalem—in one of the Peræan towns we may suppose. The notes of such an address—or rather the quoted words of the Lord in it—still bearing some of the traces of having been an address, are to be found in Luke's Gospel (xvii. 22-xviii. 8). There is a sermonic expansion among the sayings (xvii. 31-33). And the parable of the Unjust Judge with which it ends, was only quoted here by the speaker as a proof of the need for constant prayer in view of the serious nature of the times. It was doubtless related on another occasion by Jesus. The two verses with which it ends here in Luke are apparently the preacher's expansion. Silas belonged to the circle of the disciple John, and these words are reminiscent of the book of Revelation, which came from that circle, perhaps even from Silas himself. Luke would naturally question one who thus showed that he had followed Jesus, and from him he may have got some of the special sayings which are recorded in his Gospel. This parable of the Unjust Judge is kin to others of an Ebionitic tendency— parables cherished by the Jewish-Christian party in Jerusalem. Silas was a Jew, and, with all his prophetism, not without reverence and love for the old Jewish Scriptures. Parables like the Rich Man and Lazarus, in which Moses is honoured, even the Wily Steward, may have come from Silas. And while he, too, may have remembered the parable of the Pharisee and the Tax-gatherer, he would also cherish the word about the old wine being better than the new. The evangelical character of the parables of the Pharisee and the Taxgatherer, the Duty-bound Slave, the Lost Coin, and the Prodigal Son would point to the same source— Silas the evangelist, who had been so long associated with Paul, and who preached the Gospel after the same manner. To Silas we may, perhaps, assign these special fragments of the Gospel tradition (xvii. 22-xviii. 14, xvi. 19-31, xvi. 1-9, v. 39, xvii, 7-10, xv. 8-32). It is noticeable that all except one occur close together in Luke's Gospel.

Of course, from Paul too he would have heard fragments of the Gospel tradition, but Paul was hardly an eye-witness. At the same time, with this equipment, Luke would be able himself to relate much of the Gospel story, when he spoke for Christ throughout the Churches. Already he must have begun to collect the reminiscences of Jesus. For it is likely of Luke that Paul spoke when he said, "his praise in the Gospel is all over the Churches." And this referred to the days of his witnessing in Philippi and the Greek Churches. It was the memorable journey up to Jerusalem, however, that gave Luke his best opportunity.

For, when they landed at Cæsarea, they stayed a few nights with Philip the evangelist, another

of the Seventy, not impossibly the disciple of
that name. Philip's interest was in the Samaritans
among whom he laboured; and when he spoke his
reminiscences of Jesus, it would be Jesus' interest
in the Samaritans he would recall. Telling of his
own summons to service first—" Follow me ; and
let the dead bury their dead," a word which tradition
says was spoken to "Philip"—he would tell next
of the sending of the Seventy, of their joyful return,
and of the great promise about power to tread
on scorpions and over all the power of the enemy
and over spirits,—a promise which he had seen
fulfilled in his desert experiences, in his fight with
Simon Magus, and in his successful contest with
unclean spirits as he preached the kingdom and the
Name (Acts viii. 5-40). It was doubtless he from
whom Luke got the parable of the Good Samaritan ;
the story of the Samaritan village that refused to
take Jesus in, and of the gentle forbearing spirit of
Jesus in the face of this hardness of heart ; and the
incident of the cleansing of the ten lepers, one only
of whom returned to give thanks to Jesus, and he a
Samaritan (xvii. 11-19). But the greater part of his
story is recorded all together in Luke (ix. 51-x. 37).

It may be, too, that Philip's daughters had some
reminiscences to give of the women believers.
Jesus did not always receive a cold and hostile
reception, and the story which follows immediately
upon the narrative of Philip, the story of Martha
and Mary, may be a recollection of theirs (x. 38-42).

When at length Paul's company set out from
Cæsarea for Jerusalem, they made it a two days'
journey, and halted the first night at the house of
Mnason, " a disciple of the beginning "—that is,
probably, a follower of Jesus—settled now, very

likely, in the town of Lydda. It was a long day's journey; friends had come with him to introduce him to the host, and it must have been late at night when they knocked at the door of Mnason. When they excused themselves for their untimely intrusion, this old disciple, with his lamp lit and his loins girded, would smilingly pardon their lateness, and proceed to excuse himself for having so little to set before them, recalling Jesus' parable about the friend who had to borrow three loaves at midnight to tide over the unexpected visit of a late-arriving guest. This parable is recorded immediately after the narrative of Philip and his daughters. Then, as he bustled about to serve his guests, he would make light of it, recalling the Master's own promise that He would gird Himself to serve the servants whom He found faithful when He returned. As they talked together of what they had heard from the lips of Philip about the sending of the Seventy, Mnason would add some details of Jesus' instructions to them when they were sent forth, and from him, as it seems to us, would come the striking parables of Jesus' farewell address to the Galileans as He set out for Jerusalem. The word about the girded loins and the burning light recalls the parable of the Ten Virgins. There is also a word about the tenderly careful justice that will discriminate between the ignorantly and the deliberately neglectful, in the apportionment of punishment. Possibly from this rich man, too, comes the episode of the man who interrupted with the request that Jesus should become an arbitrator in a property dispute between brothers. He would tell how Jesus thrust the request aside with the brusqueness of one preparing for a tragic adventure, and recalled His hearers to the stern realities of the moment by the grim story of the Rich Fool.

But the main subject of the talk in Mnason's house that night would be concerning the unbreakable determination of his chief guest, Paul, to go up to Jerusalem, in spite of all the warnings he received, and Mnason would recall how Jesus also sternly set His face to go on a similar journey. Bonds and imprisonment awaited Paul. Was it not on Jesus' Passion Journey that He described life as a road leading to a judgment-seat ? And when Mnason heard Paul vehemently repeating his determination to go on, in spite of the kind hearts that sought to keep him back, it would be this old man, eagerly waiting for his Lord's return, who recalled the words of sublime daring spoken by the Master in similar circumstances : " I am come to throw fire on the earth. Would it were already burning ! . . . I have a baptism to be baptised with ! How am I straightened till it be accomplished ! (xi. 5-8, xii. 2-9, 11-21, 35-59).

Next day they arrived in the Holy City, and were introduced to James the brother of the Lord, and the Apostolic circle. How rich the opportunity that here presented itself to Luke ! Here are the very men who companied most closely with the Lord through all His ministry.

It seems likely that he obtained one or two priceless possessions in Jerusalem ; he may have seen Matthew's diary, and received a copy of the first rough draft of it for himself. The genealogy of Jesus he may have got from the Holy Family. But it could not have been till he reached Rome that he obtained Mark's Gospel : for it was not written until some years after that.

But here in Jerusalem he was at the very heart
of things, and how full the closing pages of Luke's
Gospel are of details of those tragic closing days!
May it not be Matthew or Matthew's friends who
recalled the story of Zacchæus, another taxgatherer
like himself, who was won by the Master down in
Jericho on the eve of His setting out up that steep road
that was to lead to Calvary (xix. 1-10)? Here in
Jerusalem he may have heard the definite prediction
about the fall of the City repeated (xix. 41-44).
But the main body of the special facts recorded by
Luke in this part of his Gospel seem to point in one
definite direction for their source. It is Luke who
names the two disciples who were sent to prepare
the Upper Room (xxii. 8); and there are added
facts about the Last Supper (xxii. 15f., 24-27, 28f.,
31f., 35-38); there is a word in Gethsemane (xxii. 53),
there is the Lord's look on Peter in Caiaphas' judgment hall (xxii. 61) and the details of the accusation
(xxiii. 2); there are words spoken from the Cross
(" Father forgive them," xxiii. 34), and to the dying
thief (xxiii. 39-43); there is Peter's visit to the empty
tomb (xxiv. 12). To these we may add the suppression
of the ambitious request of Salome and her sons.
Do these things not all point to Peter and John and
their circle as the probable informants? In " Ye
are they who have continued with me in my temptations," we have the recalling of a magnanimous
word which seems to counterbalance the dubious
note in " Can ye drink of my cup? " Similarly we
may set against the rebuke of " To sit on my right
hand and on my left is not mine to give," the word,
" I appoint unto you a kingdom " which a heart,
sore about this rebuke, would fondly cherish. " I
am among you as he that serveth," recalls the washing

of the disciples' feet which is recorded in John's Gospel alone. " Simon, Simon, behold, Satan hath desired you," must have come from the inner circle of the two or three who were Jesus' immediate companions on the way to Gethsemane. And who would remember that look in the house of Caiaphas but Peter, or John, who was also an onlooker ? Who could repeat the words from the Cross but one who stood by ? Surely the witness who often spoke about Jesus' " hour " and " the power of darkness " (Fourth Gospel) would be the one who remembered the word He spoke in the garden to the mob. From John, too, Luke may have got some of the sayings of the Baptiser. Had not John been a disciple of the prophet ?

But there are tales which women would have a special interest in remembering—the adulteress in the Temple court (a Lucan fragment possibly, though preserved only in the Fourth Gospel), the weeping women on the way to Calvary ; or in forgetting—Salome's false step in her eagerness about her sons. These suggest that Luke may have had interviews with those ministering women, some of whom no doubt were still with the first followers in Jerusalem—Salome, Mary the mother of Jesus, Mary Magdalene, Susanna, and Joanna the wife of Chuza, Herod's steward; the latter two are named by Luke alone. The consistent tradition of the Church has been that the woman who anointed Jesus' feet in Galilee was Mary Magdalene. If Joanna was the wife of the courtier whose son Jesus raised from dangerous illness, would she not have an interest in preserving the hearsay about His doings at Nain, an incident not unlike her own experience ? But above all, from whom would he get the entrancing stories of Jesus' infancy and boyhood, if not from this same circle who gathered about the mother of our Lord ? They are just the stories women would remember, and Mary is the central figure in them. Indeed some of them seem to come from Mary's own lips. Who but the weak and happy mother, her mind all wrapped in holy dreams about her infant's future, and all the wide and starry sky outside the stable peopled for her with angels that night, would have cherished the story of the simple shepherds who came in to see her babe ? Who but she would have treasured the tale of the Twelve-year-old in the Temple ? Does not Luke almost in so many words tells us they came to him from her ? Whether directly or indirectly matters not. That twice repeated word : " But Mary kept all these things and pondered them in her heart " is the plainest possible indication of their source.

IV

Only one last group of fragments of the special traditions of Luke's Gospel remain to be accounted for, those which gather round Herod and his court. Joanna, the wife of Chuza, would have access to the gossip of the court ; but was there no one else to whom Luke might have been indebted ? When Luke left the holy city with the prisoner Paul, he came to Cæsarea ; and there, during Paul's long and tedious confinement, Luke seems to have been his attendant. Many a coming and going between Paul's friends in Antioch and the prison in Cæsarea there must have been. And it is quite obvious that Luke was very specially acquainted with the great leaders in this circle of Paul's old friends. The book of Acts affords frequent proof of this. When he gives a list of the Seven whom the Apostles appointed to look after the interests of the widows of the Hellenists, there is one whose native place he mentions : " Nicolas, a proselyte of Antioch." Luke never describes a man without a reason. And in many cases it is because they are among the eye-witnesses on whom he was dependent for the facts. In this case it seems probable, however, that it was for details of the story of Stephen he has to thank Nicolas. Nicolas gave his name afterwards to a very libertarian view of Christianity. He himself may not be responsible for the extreme conduct of the Nicolaitans ; but his way of putting things may have given rise to the sect. Cherishing far-reaching views of Christian liberty, he would no doubt be an ardent follower of Stephen, and to him Luke may have been indebted for the very full account of Stephen's speech.

But there are two other words in Acts which may help us in our search. " Now they who were scattered abroad upon the persecution which arose about Stephen travelled as far as Phœnicia and Cyprus and Antioch, preaching the word to none but to Jews only. But some of them were men of Cyprus and Cyrene, who, when they were come to Antioch, spoke to the Greeks, preaching the Lord Jesus, and the hand of the Lord was with them, and a great number believed and turned to the Lord " (xi. 19). And later we read : " Now there were in the church that was in Antioch certain prophets and teachers, as Barnabas, and Simeon, that was called Niger, and Lucius of Cyrene, and Manaen who had been brought up with Herod the

Tetrarch, and Saul " (Acts xiii. 1).   From Barnabas
and from Simeon Niger (if he was Simon of Cyrene)
Luke may have heard fragments of the Gospel
story.   But to one of the names Luke here attaches
a statement of extraordinary interest—Manaen,
who had been brought up with Herod the tetrarch.
Here is one of the leading Christian teachers in the
Church at Antioch, who in his younger days was
foster-brother to the Herod who was contemporary
with Jesus.   A young lad, brought up in the royal
palace of Herod the Great as playmate and companion to young Antipas, and now a Christian teacher
—surely a romance full of wonder must lie hidden
in the reference here !   How does Luke know about
him ?   Did he meet him, and hear his story from his
own lips, in Antioch or Cæsarea ?   It must be to
him we are indebted for most of the special information Luke has to give about the court of Antipas.
For it is not merely outward facts that are given
here, but information as to Herod's feelings and
wishes such as only an intimate companion would
have known.   When the rumour of the doings of
Jesus disturbed the palace, Herod, thinking it was
the ghost of John the Baptist, " was perplexed "
(ix. 7) ;   and " he desired to see Jesus " (ix. 9).
Then during the trial in Jerusalem we are told that
" Herod was exceeding glad (relieved) when he saw
Jesus," and " he set Jesus at naught, and mocked "
(xxiii. 8, 11).   We are reminded there also that
" Herod had been at enmity with Pilate and they
were now made friends."   This picture of the
craven, ghost-haunted creature who " *wished* to
kill " Jesus in Galilee (xiii. 31), leering now with
relief writ all over his debauched face when he
sees the prisoner, bound and scourged, standing in

silence before him in Jerusalem, is to be found only in Luke's Gospel.

What, then, of Manaen ?   Can we find the clue to his story ?

When Herod the Great, father of the Tetrarch, was a boy, he was met one day on the street by a member of the Essenes, that remarkable group of ascetics who fraternised as a colony in the Jordan valley.   The holy man laid his hand on the princeling and predicted that he would become king of the Jews.   The prophecy came true, and the monarch, whose vanity had been gratified, sought to honour and befriend the seer.   Josephus, the historian who tells the story, says the man's name was Manaen. It must be this man to whom the Talmudic legend refers, which says that Menahem (the Hebrew form of the name) a leading rabbi, entered the household service of the king.   Does it not seem likely that it was this Manaen who had procured some younger relative of his, bearing the same uncommon name, as a foster-brother for Herod the Great's young son ?

These two foster brothers grew to manhood, and in course of time Herod Antipas became tetrarch, a strange, lustful creature, crafty, cruel, capricious, effeminate, treacherous, ostentatious, cowardly, vain aping foreign culture, building cities like Tiberias after a Greek model, pretending to be religious, or at least interested in the Jewish religion, barbarous untamed, superstitious to the core.   We wonder sometimes what influence Manaen had upon him, or he on Manaen.   Did the lad from the strict Jewish family influence the king for good, or did Antipas corrupt Manaen ?   Was Manaen present in the palace gardens when the shaggy man with the cloak of camel's hair and the leathern girdle stalked in and confronted the king, and with outstretched rebuking finger said, " It is not lawful for thee to have thy brother's wife " ? Was it Manaen's hand that was the restraining hand working against the influence of Herodias, when the king arrested the Baptiser, but feared at first to put him to death ? Was it Manaen's influence that made the king's conscience tender so that he sought interviews with John in prison, in a vain endeavour to find peace for his guilty soul ? Whether through the healing of the courtier's son (recorded in the Fourth Gospel) or in some other way, the influence of the new " Prophet " had reached the precincts of the royal palace in Tiberias, compelling idle, light-minded aristocrats to chatter. Herod had by this time succumbed to the wiles of Herodias, and destroyed John. We can see him wandering about the palace in Tiberias, shuddering at the winds that moaned along its corridors ; wandering in his garden, and starting at every dark bush, as though it were that hairy-mantled prophet confronting him once again ; shrinking before the gloating eyes of the triumphant Herodias ; sitting down to his meals abstracted, preoccupied, while the gay courtiers prattled their light table-talk. And one day it was Jesus who was the subject of their witticisms. Some stray word had arrested the taciturn monarch's attention. They were trying to account for this Jesus in their indifferent way. " A new prophet," said one. " One of the old prophets," contradicted another. " Which ? " asked a third. " Elias," suggested a fourth. Then, after a pause someone capped the guessing with a random jest : " John the Baptist risen again ! " Suddenly they were all startled by a cry from the head of the table. At once all eyes were riveted on the king. He must have looked the picture of terror—straining eyes, lips drawn and twitching, nostrils quivering and dilated, the blood fled from his cheeks, as clutching the table he shouted: "He whom I murdered? . . . John! . . . Yes, it is he!—risen from the dead. And the powers of evil are urging on their attack on me through him." So the rank superstition of the King translated the horrible dreams of a troubled conscience that had vexed his midnight slumbers.

> In the night, in the night
> When thou liest alone,
> Ah! the ghosts that make moan
> From the days that are sped:
> The old dreams, the old deeds,
> The old wound that still bleeds,
> And the face of the dead,
>   In the night.

And to some intimate he expressed a wish to kill Jesus. There can be little doubt it was Manaen. But Manaen was troubled too. All his uneasiness at the contrast between the stern ascetic life of the Pharisees and Essenes, to whom his family belonged, and the luxury and debauch of the palace, had come to a head through the influence of this great Soul of purity who was making His presence felt in all the cities round the Lake. He called some of his Pharisee friends, and sent them with a secret message to Jesus, bidding Him begone for His life from the neighbourhood of Tiberias (Luke xiii. 31). His interest in the prophet had previously prompted him to try to deter him from going up to Jerusalem, and the menace that was threatening there (xiii. 1f.). But this was a more imminent danger still. Jesus, however, treated it with fearless contempt. Manaen had been terrified by Jesus' stern insistence on repentence, when he heard Him talk (Luke xiii. 2-5). The parable of the fig-tree that was a cumberer of the ground had stung him to the quick (xiii. 6-9). Yet he had witnessed also the compassion of Jesus (xiii. 10-17), and had taken courage and hope from the parables of the grain of mustard seed and the leaven ; for his soul was like that leaven—in a state of upheaval and ferment (xiii. 18-21). Nevertheless he had heard Him say that the need for entering in at the narrow gate was inexorable, else some day he might find himself standing outside a closed door, vainly seeking entrance on the heavenly life he had spurned (xiii. 22-30). And now, when this daring answer had come back to the palace concerning Herod's threat, it was a wholesome breath blowing into the fœtid air of the place. The great Teacher and Healer with the tender heart feared not the face of man. Greater than John the Baptist—in His own right, this man was a king ! Manaen was faced with a stern alternative. Either he must live on in the company of his awakened conscience, or cut himself forever free from all the luxury and debauchery of the palace. He came to the only right decision, and his soul reached peace.

He entertained the Rabbi in his house beyond the confines of the city, perhaps at the hot springs of Hamath, near the royal baths. It was he who related to Luke Jesus' table-talk (xiv. 1-24). And then, when Jesus had set out upon the road again, he heard and answered the great call to decision (xiii. 25-27). And very probably it was from him Luke heard the parables about counting the cost —those vivid pictures of the derelict, half-built house, and the monarch with the ill-equipped armies

setting out for war. Though the end of his life
in the royal palace had come, he may have been
present to witness the insults of the mocking king
when his new Master stood on trial at the last. In a
few brief weeks Herod, the self-styled king, received
a crushing defeat at the hands of the Arab king,
the father of the wife he had wronged ; and his
ancient stronghold on the Dead Sea shore was sacked
and burned with fire. But Manaen had heard
another call to war:

> The Son of God goes forth to war,
>   A kingly crown to gain ;
> His blood-red banner streams afar ;
>   Who follows in His train ?

And Manaen had exchanged his allegiance. He
was taking part in the founding of the Gentile
church at Antioch when Herod set out on his
ill-fated journey to Rome. Cringing there abjectly
before Caesar's throne, the wretched Herod had
begged for the very title which he had flung at Christ
in mockery. Refused and banished into exile—
thrown up to rot on the rocks of time—he must
have realised at last—too late—that the voice that
had troubled his conscience was not John's voice,
but God's. As for Manaen, he had the supreme joy
of witnessing the kingdom of God growing from a
grain of mustard seed to be a mighty tree. Brought
up in a royal palace, accustomed to a soft, luxurious
mode of life, he had nevertheless laid it all aside, and
gone out to endure hardness as a good soldier of
Jesus Christ. He had become a fearless advocate
of the Crucified One, on the streets of a morally
corrupt city, one of the four largest and vilest in
the world. He had joined the Salvation Army,
counting the cost.

CHAPTER VIII

An Anonymous Book

" WHO it was that wrote the Epistle to the Hebrews God only knows." Eusebius quotes the words from the great Alexandrian, Origen. And the letter is just as titleless as it is anonymous. There is no basis for the tradition that St. Paul was the author, though the conjecture was floated early, and Western Christendom came to acquiesce in uncritical acceptance. The authority of Pope and Council, however, must give place to the authority of truth. The doubt about this tradition existed and was freely expressed before the first Christian century was ended. It found a voice for itself in all the great Christian Fathers: not Origen alone, but Clement of Rome, Tertullian, and even Jerome and Augustine. Luther voiced it; and the unanimous voice of modern Christian scholarship has turned the doubt into a practically certain negative.

" The writer cites differently," says Dean Farrar, " he writes differently; he argues differently; he thinks differently; he declaims differently; he constructs and connects his sentences differently; he builds up his paragraphs on a wholly different model. St. Paul is constantly mingling two constructions, leaving sentences unfinished, breaking into personal allusions, substituting the syllogism of passion for the syllogism of logic. The writer is never ungrammatical, he is never irregular, he is never personal, he never struggles for expression, he never loses himself in a parenthesis, he is never hurried into an anacoluthon. His style is the style of a man who thinks, as well as writes, in Greek, whereas St. Paul wrote in Greek and thought in Syriac."

There are two different types of logical mind, the type that thinks in antithesis, states clear-cut contraries and contradictions; and the type that treats thought as something that develops and progresses organically. These types are well represented in St. Paul and the writer of this letter. They spring from different temperaments, the temperament of moral intensity, and that of philosophic repose. There is no clearer conclusion of literary criticism than that St. Paul was not the author of the so-called Epistle to the Hebrews.

It is a fascinating document, written by a forceful and able mind. It turned up first in the city of Rome—as, according to a letter of Clement of Rome, it would seem—within thirty years after it was written. There must have been people alive who knew the author. Why is the name withheld? The letter bears on the face of it that it was sent to a definite destination; and the author writes as one well-known to the recipients. It is not as though false authorship was claimed for it, at the outset. The earliest suggestions made are but guesses. It is the unique case of a nameless letter, author and destination of which are alike unknown. Yet when men began to quote it first, both must have been known. The mystery raises in us the suspicion that the name of the writer has been deliberately suppressed. And we wonder why.

Hidden Romance of the New Testament

I

Something can be learned about *the author* from the merest surface examination of the document. Undoubtedly it is a convert from Judaism, not from Paganism, who writes. It is perhaps the most convincing attempt that has ever been made to show that Christianity is the true and only fulfilment of the ancient Jewish faith. From the references to the persecution of the Chasidim and the sufferings of the patriots of the Maccabean days (xi. 38), the writer has obvious sympathy with those defenders of the ancient covenant, and may have belonged to them by descent. The author is obviously a Christian who had never lost the longing to win the Jewish race for Christ.

A second undoubted fact is that the author was acquainted with, and indeed accepted the fundamental truth of, a certain type of Greek philosophy which was current at the time. It was a philosophy which owed its origin to Plato, and which was developed later in the Jewish University of Alexandria, notably by Philo. Yet this letter is not the work of a strenuous advocate of that view, only of one who had had intercourse with Philonists, for there is, as Bruce points out, " a very free and independent use of words and ideas hailing from that quarter." This philosophy was that view of the world which said that the visible created things are only the appearances ; the shadows of invisible spiritual realities. The things which we see are fleeting and transitory ; the unseen realities are eternal. This distinction of shadow and substance runs throughout the thought of the epistle. The ancient tabernacle was the shadow of the invisible Temple, the building not made with hands, the worshipping fellowship of all believers. Jerusalem was no continuing city, it was a type of the heavenly city, the new Jerusalem, whose Builder and Maker was God. The ancient sacrifices were but symbolic of the eternal sacrifice made once for all by Christ. The long succession of the Jewish priesthood was just the shadow of the eternal priesthood—after the order of Melchisedec, who was without father, without mother, without beginning or ending of days—the eternal priesthood which was at length perfectly and finally fulfilled in Christ.

The author, then, was a Jewish Christian, deeply skilled in the ancient Hebrew Scriptures, a highly-cultured mind, acquainted with what was best in one of the most influential philosophies of the age. We gather also that the author held a leading place in the community to which the letter was sent, was for some reason absent from them, and was longing to be back among them again (xiii. 18f.).

A pathetic feature of the document, too, is that the writer assumes the attitude and outlook of a pilgrim, a wanderer, a refugee, conscious of possessing no earthly resting-place, consciously bearing the reproach of Christ (xiii. 13f.), one who has had to seek safety in flight (vi. 18). These things are painted rather by suggestion than directly; and along with them there is the constant recurrence of nautical and semi-nautical terms, the fruit of the experience of one who had done much voyaging, and possibly also the experience of one whose occupation led to contact with sea-faring folk. It is immediately after the writer speaks of us " who have fled for refuge to lay hold upon the hope set before us," that the figure is used of hope as " an anchor of the soul, both sure and steadfast, and entering into that which is within the veil." It is this writer who quotes as an example of faith the building of a boat (xi. 7.) And how often is use made of words like " holding fast " (iii. 6, 14 ; iv. 14 ; vi. 18), or " drawing near " (vii. 19), almost in the sense of a ship approaching land (x. 22). We read also of " drifting " from a course (ii. 1), as a metaphor for faith in danger ; of being " swept about," as in a current (xiii. 9) ; of " loosing from the moorings of death " (xiii. 20), as a description of the resurrection ; of " shortening of sail " (x. 38, 39), as a description of hesitation or timidity in religion ; of " driving on," or " being borne on " (vi. 1) unto perfection ; of " casting away " our confidence (x. 35), as if it were ballast ; of " looking " with the fixed gaze of the pilot (xi. 26) ; of " being on the outlook " (xi. 10) as if for sight of the approaching haven ; of " seeing from afar " (xi. 13), as if one had caught sight of the shore ; of " greeting the promises " (xi. 13), a word reminiscent of friends on deck, waving to friends on the shore ; of " holding on one's course, as seeing the invisible " (xi. 27). These and other phrases and metaphors have about them the salt tang of much sea-faring.

Another curious feature of the document may be noted ere we pass from this preliminary enquiry about the writer. The author often talks in the first person singular, often says " I "—an indication that one mind is mainly responsible for the work. But sometimes we come across a first person plural— " we," where it cannot mean that the writer is claiming association with the readers, nor yet talking with editorial dignity, but that there was another at least, with whom the writer was in constant consultation when preparing the letter.

An Anonymous Book

II

It may carry us a further stage in the solution of the mystery, if we turn now to make enquiry of the letter as to the identity of *the recipients*. The title " Epistle to the Hebrews " is as old as the first recognition of the letter in the New Testament Canon. But it is not from the hand of the author ; probably the contents of the letter suggested it to some transcriber. The validity of the title has been challenged, but not seriously. It has been thought that the phrase " falling away from the living God " implies that the recipients were in danger of lapsing back into their earlier paganism. But the whole argument of the Epistle, the contrasting of Christianity with Judaism, would be an irrelevancy, unless the danger was that of a relapse to Judaism. Why be at such pains to prove that Christianity was the perfection of Judaism if the danger was a lapse not only from Christianity but from Judaism itself ? What the writer fears is a falling from the living God of progressive revelation to the God of dead tradition. While the writer recognises Christianity as a universal religion, there are phrases which suggest that the recipients were exclusively Jews. When the writer tells that Christ did not identify Himself with angels in order to rescue them—instead of saying it was with the race of men He identified Himself, he says it was with the " seed of Abraham " (ii. 16). And when the exhortation is addressed to the readers, " let us go forth unto Him without the camp " (xiii. 13), the implication is that the recipients were Jews who were being called upon to cut themselves free from Judaism. It was therefore to a Jewish community the letter was sent.

11

But was it to *all* Hebrew Christians everywhere throughout the world, or only to a definitely localised group ? Once more the answer seems quite certain. It was to some particular local community of Hebrew Christians ; and certain facts about them are clear. The great salvation which had " at the first been spoken through the Lord was confirmed unto us by them that heard " (ii. 3). They were not Jews who had themselves been eye-witnesses and ear-witnesses of Jesus, but their first teachers had been such. Yet the recipients still belonged to the generation that had listened to these teachers, though it is obvious that they had been Christians for some considerable time now, and that these first teachers were probably dead (xiii. 7). " For," says the writer, " when by this time ye ought to be teachers, ye have need again that some one teach you the rudiments of the first principles of the oracles of God " (v. 12)—a sentence which not only proves that the recipients had been Christians for a time, but that they were beginning to lose grasp of the essentials of the faith, in some measure. Not that they were apostates : the writer can still describe them as " holy brethren, partakers of a heavenly calling " (iii. 1), and " not of them that shrink back into perdition, but of them that have faith, . . ." (x. 39). And the writer can recall their " work and the love which they showed toward His (Christ's) Name for that they ministered unto the saints and still do minister " (vi. 10).

Yet the author is aware that they were in danger of drifting away (ii. 1) ; of being neglectful (ii. 3) ; of developing the hard and evil heart of unbelief (iii. 8, 12) ; of contempt and despite (x. 29) ; of refusing to listen to the voice of the Christian revelation (xii. 25); of spiritual dullness (v. 11); of waxing weary and fainting (xii. 3); of shrinking from the reproach of Christ (xiii. 13); of disaffection (xiii. 17); of crucifying the Lord afresh (vi. 6). It is not easy to specify with any precision what particular form the apostasy of which they were in danger seemed likely to take, for the verse which speaks of diverse and strange teachings, and of meats, is one of the most difficult to interpret in the whole epistle. But probably they were in danger of being drawn away by the revival of Judaism which was following the diffusion of the Alexandrian teaching, a Judaism which tempted them to surrender belief in the historical Jesus, speciously suggesting they might retain the Christ-idea (xiii. 9).

More interesting still for our present purpose are certain other facts about this community which we can gather from the letter. Their first reception of Christianity seems to have been accompanied by the spiritual phenomena which we are familiar with in revival movements (ii. 4). And these again were followed by a certain nagging opposition on the part of those who refused to be persuaded by the new propaganda, and apparently also by state officials. " Call to remembrance the former days, in which, after ye were enlightened, ye endured a great conflict of sufferings; partly being made a gazing stock, both by reproaches and afflictions; and partly, becoming partakers with them that were so used. For ye both had compassion on them that were in bonds, and took joyfully the spoiling of your possessions " (x. 32f.). This great initial spiritual awakening had made a commotion in the place; the believers had suffered mockery, insult, rough handling; and the legal authorities had apparently interfered, and put a veto on the movements of some of them, including, according to some MSS., the writer ; and had even distrained some of their property, as a fine for the disturbance, probably.

To this must be added a still more interesting reference : " Ye have not yet resisted unto blood, striving against the iniquity " (xii. 4). Some commentators refuse to admit that this is a reference to the persecution. " Striving against sin " is to them the stumbling-block. They would take it to mean, " ye have not yet resisted sin in deadly earnest." But the context surely demands a different interpretation. Just before these words, the author has referred to the enduring of the Cross, and the gainsaying of sinners by Jesus, and immediately after the words, proceeds to speak of enduring chastening. So that we are entitled to infer that these words reveal the writer's knowledge that there had been no martyrdoms in this first persecution, bad though it was. " Striving against sin " is another way of saying " enduring the gainsaying of sinners " —the " wearing persecution of taunt and sneer, of social ostracism, and petty annoyances."

It is evident also that the writer is addressing an exhortation to the recipients, in view of a time, which seemed imminent, when they might be called upon to put their faith to the dread proof of martyrdom. " Ye see the day drawing nigh " (x. 25), a day in which there is to be another " shaking of heaven and earth " (xii. 26). This seems evident also from the number of cases of ancient and horrible martyrdom, yet faithful endurance, which the writer quotes for their encouragement and example.

An Anonymous Book

One other inference may be made about this community. When the writer urges them "not to forsake the assembling of ourselves together" (x. 24f), the meaning apparently is, not that they were to maintain their Christian fellowship in general, but that they were to stick to their own congregation. The letter is addressed, therefore, not to all the Hebrew Christians in one town even, but to one little company, mainly Jewish, one of the many little house-churches, in fact, which were so characteristic of the early beginnings of Christianity. They were evidently a small and homogenous community, all the members of which came under the same description (v. 12). They were Jews, and it seems as if part of their persecution had been from the unbelieving Jews in the same town. They are exhorted to go forth unto Christ without the camp, bearing His reproach, for He also had suffered without the gate (xiii. 12, 13), as though their stand for Christ had alienated them from the Ghetto in this town. And while they did at one time show compassion to Christian leaders in bonds (x. 33f), even as Christians in Rome had befriended Paul the prisoner, yet it seems also as if they had failed to pay respect to these venerable teachers on some occasion, even as the Jewish Christians in Rome had failed to stand by Paul at his first trial in the Roman capital (*cf.* Heb. xiii. 3. 7 with 2 Tim. iv. 16).

The letter, then, was written to one little gathering of Jewish Christians who met in a certain house in a certain town ; a community with which the writer was once intimately associated in the early days of their Christian life, sharing indeed their experiences in a conspicuous degree.

III

With all this definite and detailed information about the history and circumstances of the congregation before us, can we identify the town or the community ? Five towns have been suggested at one time or another : Jerusalem, Antioch, Cæsarea, Alexandria, Rome. Let us examine the claims of these cities in the light of the information just presented.

Can we say of the Christians in Jerusalem that none of them had been hearers of Jesus ? (ii. 3). The Hebrew-Christian community in Jerusalem at the beginning contained many who had themselves heard the Lord. The Church we are seeking to identify had been founded by Apostolic missionaries (ii. 3, xiii. 7). It had been a distinct event (x. 32), and these things are not true of the Church in Jerusalem. This congregation had not as yet done much, if anything, in the way of propagating the Faith (v. 12) ; whereas the Jerusalem Church had already done a great deal in the way of teaching others. This Church had taken its share in Christian hospitality, in ministering to the saints (vi. 10) : they had a sufficient share of this world's goods to have suffered spoliation (x. 34). The Christians in Jerusalem were poor and had to be supported. Further, Greek is undoubtedly the original language of this Epistle. If the Epistle had been sent to Hebrew Christians in Jerusalem, it would have been written first in Syriac. That it was sent to Greek-speaking Jews of the Dispersion is borne out by the fact that it is always the LXX. that is quoted. Moreover, it is not true of the early Jerusalem Church that it had " not yet resisted unto blood." And a writer to these Judaistic Christians of

Jerusalem could not have written so disparagingly of the ancient ceremonial (ix. 10, xii. 18). We might add that Timothy's coming (xiii. 23) would not be regarded as an event by the Jerusalem Christians.

Was it Antioch ? The supposed authorship by Barnabas has suggested this town. No doubt Barnabas was a Hebrew Christian, an educated man, a Levite, familiar with the ancient Jewish ceremonies. But a Levite could never have so ignored the Temple ritual. A certain resemblance between " Hebrews " and the so-called " Epistle of Barnabas " has in part been made the basis for this identification of authorship. But the epistle of Barnabas is a late document, not written by Barnabas at all. In all probability Barnabas had attended the University at Tarsus, where he would come under the influence of the Stoic philosophy, not the Alexandrian, with which the writer of " Hebrews " was familiar. And if the author had been this man of Apostolic rank and influence, it would be strange indeed if the fact had been forgotten. But apart from the identification of the author, it may be pointed out that the Church at Antioch had been one of the great centres of early Christian propaganda. They would hardly be reproached for not by this time being teachers of others. And it was largely a Gentile Church, and its missionary work was directed to Gentiles. Nor can we point to any persecution of the Church in Antioch, such as this congregation endured.

The claims of Cæsarea to be the destination of this letter are almost negligible. They have apparently been put forward partly on the ground that Luke was the author, writing a free translation of the thoughts of Paul, perhaps during his imprisonment there, or soon after. But we have already seen how little the thought resembles Paul's. And Luke the Gentile could not have the familiarity with, or interest in, the ancient Jewish ritual which this writer displays. And the little we know of the Christians in Cæsarea militates against the theory that they had endured the experience which the recipients of this letter had suffered, or that the character of this church was at all like that of the congregation whose identity we are attempting to trace.

As for Alexandria, this letter was much appreciated there, but the great Alexandrian Origen says the author was quite unknown. Had it been sent there, it is extremely improbable that the name of its sender would have been so completely forgotten. There could not have been such a violent break in the history of the Alexandrian Church as this implies. Indeed, the Alexandrians were under the impression that its recipients were Palestinian Jews ; not that they had any tradition to that effect ; it is merely their interpretation of the facts contained in the letter. Alexandria has been suggested because of the undoubtedly happy conjecture that Apollos was the author. But the facts of Apollos' history are all against the view that he had experienced an enlightenment in which there were outward manifestations of the Spirit (ii. 4, x. 32), when Christianity came to Alexandria. Apollos was only a half Christian, a follower of John the Baptiser, when he came to Ephesus. He certainly did not receive the faith from ear-witnesses of the Lord in Alexandria. Indeed his enlighteners in Ephesus were not ear-witnesses of the Lord. We read of a persecution of Jews in Alexandria in the year 38 A.D., but they were not Christian Jews.

An Anonymous Book

IV

The claims of Rome remain to be considered. And the first cursory glance at the letter reveals something which awakens our interest. Just before the parting benediction with which the writer ends the letter, come the words " They of Italy salute you." And at once our conjectures are confined to a narrow range; either the writer is writing from Italy, or to some place in Italy. But if the writer had been in Italy at the time, it would not be the greetings of the Christians of all that country that would have been sent, but only those of the particular town in Italy from which the letter was written. The conclusion that the writer is beyond Italy is the more probable, and the form of the words themselves bear this out. They mean " those away from, or hailing from, Italy." When the same word is used elsewhere in similar phrases in the New Testament, it seems to have this implication (*cf*. Matt. xv. 1 ; Acts xxi. 27, xxiv. 18). But it is clear also that there were certain Italian Christians in the writer's company when the letter was sent. And why send *their* greetings more than those of any of the other Christians of the place ? There can be only one reason. The letter was being sent to a community in Italy. The fact that there are Italian Christians associated with the writing of the letter indicates surely that the author had an Italian connection. And naturally exiled Italians in the place where the writer was would have a special interest in sending greetings to Christians in their native land. We may add here also that the reference to the possibility of Timothy's accompanying the writer on a visit to the place would have point if that town were Rome. The verse is not easy to translate with definiteness, but it is certainly not necessary to suppose that Timothy had been imprisoned *in* Rome, nor indeed that he was in prison at all. The words might mean " Know ye that our brother Timothy is loosed from his charge," (or from some task he had in hand), " with whom, if he come soon, I will see you." The interest of a congregation in Rome concerning a visit of Timothy is easily understood. He had been there a considerable time with Paul. Was it to the Hebrew Christians in Rome then, that this letter was sent ? The first Christians we hear of in Italy were in Rome. And the first time we ever hear of the letter, it is in the possession of Christians in that city. Clement of Rome makes frequent use of it as early as 95 A.D.

Here, however, a question we have not hitherto considered thrusts itself before us. When was the letter written ? It must have been a considerable time before 95 A.D., since Clement quotes it as a document whose authority was recognised It would seem, too, that although it is the ritual of the Tabernacle, not of the Temple in Jerusalem, that the writer refers to, nevertheless the Temple was still standing, and its sacrifices still in vogue. It is true that the pious compilers of the Mishna, down in Jamnia, after the fall of Jerusalem in 70 A.D., did regard it as a sacred duty to preserve minute records of the Temple ritual, to talk of it as still authoritative, and to expect its restoration. But a Jewish *Christian* would hardly talk as this author does, unless the Temple were still standing— although perhaps there was hanging over it a menacing cloud of doom (viii. 13). Had the Temple fallen, the necessity for arguing against a lapse to Leviticism on the part of Jewish Christians would scarcely exist. Indeed, if Jerusalem had fallen, the writer could not have failed to refer to so stupendous a judgment on the ancient Hebrew ritual. It would seem, therefore, that we are led to postulate a date for the letter prior to 70 A.D. But by the year 65 A.D., the disturbances in Jerusalem had begun, which led ultimately to its overthrow. And the writer seems conscious of writing on the eve of a crisis, a day of judgment fast approaching for the Jewish people (x. 25, xii. 26f.).

A parallel is drawn in this letter between the case of the Israelites in the wilderness and the present situation. He speaks of the " day of temptation in the wilderness, when your fathers tempted me, proved me and saw my works forty years " (iii. 8f.). And the suggestion seems to be that a similar period of time had well-nigh elapsed since the day of the first manifestation of the risen Christ. This again would suggest some time not long prior to 70 A.D.

Was there ever a persecution of Christians in Rome such as is referred to in this letter ? The reign of Domitian extended from 81 to 96 A.D. And the severe policy against the Christians began in 83. But this is subsequent to the fall of the Holy City. The Neronian persecution began in 65, but there were soon many cases " unto blood " at this time. And since the writer says that those to whom the letter was sent had " not yet resisted unto blood," it must have been prior to the blood-shedding time of the Neronian persecution. A sore time of persecution was evidently approaching, but in the early part of 65 A.D., although opposition was fermenting, there had as yet been no active outbreak. This may have been the approaching persecution the writer was contemplating, but it is not the actual persecution which the letter refers to; for that took place soon after the enlightenment (x. 32). and the Neronian persecution was long after that time. Was there any persecution in Rome before the time of Nero ? Only one, and that not unto blood. We are led therefore to fix as the probable date of the writing of the letter sometime about the middle or the early part of 65 A.D. For Rome fulfils in every particular all the conditions implied in this letter. There were Hebrew Christians in Rome. Paul's letter to Rome confirms us in this. We have evidence too, that they formed a separate community in Rome. Moreover, Christianity came to Rome some considerable time before the probable date of the writing of the letter. And there were certain heterodox tendencies troubling the Christians in Rome. Paul's letter indeed informs us that the question of " meats " was one of them (*cf.* Heb. xiii. 9 with Rom. xiv.). And there was a persecution of Jewish Christians there in the early days, though not unto blood. This leads us to the story we have now to tell.

V

In the year 50 A.D. there arrives one day in the streets of Corinth a bald-headed, bandy-legged, sturdily built little man with red-lidded eyes and the marks of suffering on his face. He is a foreigner, a Jew, and he is evidently in search of a job. So at least the casual passer-by would conclude. He wanders down to the neighbourhood of the harbour, and enters the Jewish quarters, eagerly scanning the sign-boards as he goes along. At length he sees swinging above one of the doors a placard bearing the freshly-painted letters Ἀκύλα σκηνοποιός (Akyla skēnopoios). He will make enquiries here. So he approaches the bench where the owner of the shop is sitting stitching away at the canvas. "Greetings, brother," says the man in a welcoming, kindly tone: "Peace to thee!" "And to thee peace!" answers the wandering workman; "I am a tent-maker by trade. Have you any work for an extra hand?" And the man paused to scrutinise the new-comer up and down with gently smiling eyes. "I see you are a Jew, like myself," he says. "But you don't wear the zizith any more than I do. How is that?" "To be quite frank with you," answers the other, "I've given up the ancient faith. I am a follower of the Prophet whom men call the Nazarene." "Now, here is an astonishing thing," says the suddenly excited tent-maker. "It chances that I am also a follower." "And I thought," says the new comer, with a whimsical look of mingled delight and disappointment, "that the Gospel had never been in Corinth till I set foot in it to-day. But perhaps you are a stranger, too? It seems that you have recently come." "You are right," says Aquila the tent-maker. "Except for my wife and myself, I know of no other followers of the New Way here. Not many Sabbaths have passed since we came to the place. We have but recently established our business. And you are the very man I want, for the work has speedily grown to be more than I can undertake alone. You can stay. You are the first man in this place to whom we have revealed our opinions. We have kept them to ourselves. We have a reason."

"From whence, then, have you come ? " asked Paul, for it was he. "We have come from Rome, driven out by an edict of the Emperor." "But why ? " "O, why, but for being too zealous in our new faith ! " And so Paul joined himself to the tent-maker, as fellow-craftsman and friend.

The words from the Book of Acts (xviii. 1ff.) which tell us of this forgathering of Christian strangers may be recorded here : "After these things Paul departed from Athens, and came to Corinth. And he found a certain Jew named Aquila, born in Pontus, lately come from Italy, with his wife Priscilla (because that Claudius had commanded all Jews to depart from Rome), and came unto them. And because he was of the same craft, he abode with them and wrought, for by their occupation they were tent-makers. And he reasoned in the synagogue every Sabbath, and persuaded the Jews and the Greeks."

What was the reason for this command of the Emperor Claudius ? A deeply significant sentence in contemporary secular history informs us. Suetonius, the Roman historian (*Claudius*, § xxv.) writes—and betrays his half-informed indifference, when he says — "*Judæos, impulsore Chresto, assidue tumultuantes, Româ expulit*" (He—that is Claudius—expelled the Jews from Rome, because they were persistently creating disturbances, a certain Chrestus being the moving spirit). The word "Chrestus" betrays signs of imperfectly reported hearsay. It should be Christus—Christ. There can be little doubt that we are here listening to echoes of the dim story of the first moving of the Spirit of the Risen Christ, down in the Jewish Ghetto in Rome. We know that not all Jews were expelled at this time from the Imperial City, and that the edict by and by fell into abeyance. It is clear, therefore, that Aquila and Priscilla had been leaders in the new movement, since they were among the number who had been expelled. They had been eagerly trying to spread the Gospel Message among their own compatriots, and through their zeal and ability had been marked out as ringleaders. The enmity of rigid and prejudiced Jews had been stirred against them. Christ was the moving Spirit in their hearts; and the riots gathered about them as storm-centres.

We are in search for an author. Have we found him—or her? *They* are Jewish Christians. *They* became exiles from the city and the Church where their new faith began. If *they* had ever had occasion to write to their first Christian associates it would be to a community consisting mainly of Christian Jews and proselytes, and it would be to the city of Rome. *They* could recall having suffered with that church in the days following its spiritual illumination—suffered, but not to the shedding of blood. And from what we know of them elsewhere in the sacred record, their main interest was how to make the new Faith attractive to their compatriots. They seem to have agreed with Paul in his endeavour to carry the Gospel first to Jews. When he stayed with them at Corinth they probably accompanied him to the synagogue, where he argued Sabbath by Sabbath with his fellow-countrymen. And when the two accompanied Paul to Ephesus once again his first appearance was in the synagogue. And there, it is evident, Aquila and Priscilla continued to worship after Paul had gone. For when Apollos, the follower of the Baptiser, came to Ephesus from Alexandria, his addresses were delivered in the synagogue (Acts xviii. 26), and Aquila and Priscilla were among his hearers.

When we consider the other references to the canvas-worker and his wife, an interesting fact comes to light. They are mentioned some six times in the New Testament, and when the readings in the various MSS. are compared, we find that on the majority of occasions it is Priscilla or Prisca who is mentioned first. It is probably due to the longer Western Text that Aquila's name comes first when their names are first mentioned (Acts xviii. 2). Aquila certainly is never mentioned alone; and that fact by itself justifies the inference that Priscilla took an equally important part with her husband in all their Christian activity. On one, if not two, of the three occasions when Luke mentions them, Priscilla's name comes first. And of the three occasions on which Paul mentions them, only once, and there probably for reasons of etiquette, does Aquila's name come first (1 Cor. xvi. 19). It is when *their* greetings are being sent to the Church in Corinth. The other two occasions are when Paul is sending his greetings to them. And Paul, who took a severe and rigid view of the place of women in Christian assemblies, always thinks of Prisca first (Rom. xvi. 3; 2 Tim. iv. 19). It seems practically certain that she was the more forceful and brilliant personality of the two. And when Christianity began to win its way in the places where they settled, they seem to have formed a house-congregation of their own. Not immediately, indeed, in Ephesus, for not only did Paul preach the Gospel, but Apollos proclaimed the way of the Lord, in the Jewish synagogue first. When Paul returned to Ephesus some considerable time afterwards, he still, for a time, conducted his propaganda in the synagogue. And even when he was banned therefrom, it was in the class-room of Tyrannus that he continued his campaign. Aquila and Priscilla were strangers in Ephesus, of course, when the good news was first proclaimed there. But it is evident that by-and-by they became leaders of the new Christian community. For when writing to Corinth Paul says : " Aquila and Prisca, with the church that meets in their house, salute you warmly in the Lord " (1 Cor. xvi. 19).

It has been widely held in recent years that the destination of the sixteenth chapter of the letter to Rome was not Rome but Ephesus. For there Paul says : " Salute Prisca and Aquila, my fellow-workers in Christ Jesus, who have risked their lives for me ; I thank them, and not only I, but all the Gentile Churches as well " (Rom. xvi. 3f.). When Paul first met them, they were in Corinth, refugees from Rome, and they accompanied him to Ephesus, where they seem to have settled for a time at least. But further, in a greeting, in what is no doubt a genuine fragment of a letter of Paul's (2 Tim. iv. 19)—a letter sent to Timothy, who was in Ephesus—he says : " Salute Prisca and Aquila." At first sight, it would seem natural to suppose that the two had remained during all the interval, of some eight years at least, in Ephesus. But it is noteworthy that the remaining words of the verse in this latter reference are : " And the household of Onesiphorus." The probable inference is that these two had no longer a house-church there in Ephesus. May it not well have been that they had been absent from Ephesus for a considerable time, and the congregation which met in their house had been broken up ?

Certain facts strongly support this view. The edict of the Emperor Claudius, which had compelled them to leave Rome, had proved impracticable, and fallen into abeyance. Surely there must have been a strong desire in the hearts of Prisca and Aquila to revisit the home where they had first, and doubtless for long years, been citizens, and to resume the intercourse with their earliest brethren in Christ as soon as the way was clear, perhaps even to settle in their old home again. Further, when Paul mentions (Rom. xvi. 4) that they had risked their lives for him, it is almost certain that he means in Ephesus. Surely the danger which they had incurred there would be a strong reason for their quitting that city for a time. To this we shall return in the next chapter.

But let us go back now to the Epistle to the Hebrews. Have we not already seen strong reason to believe that the writer, or writers, had experienced much voyaging in their time—persons with no continuing city, frequently pilgrims and refugees? It lends considerable support to our attributing this letter to one or other of these two, to remember this. It may be a mere chance that the writer speaks of the sacred Tent, employing the word as many times as in all the rest of the New Testament, and that the veil (woven of goat's-hair canvas) is frequently spoken of, for of course a large part of the argument gathers round a comparison of the ritual of the Tabernacle with the features of the new faith. But surely there is a certain pathetic interest in the phrase with which the writer once describes the faith of Abraham— " residing in tents " (xi. 9). Frequently, too, the writer uses a word which is rare in the New Testament ($\kappa\alpha\tau\alpha\rho\tau\iota\zeta\epsilon\iota\nu$ —to repair, literally, to weave together—x. 5, xi. 3, xiii. 21

perhaps a familiar word in the writer's craft). In the peculiar word " thou shalt roll them up " (i. 12, the best attested reading), which is an unusual translation of the Hebrew Scriptures quoted, we may have another hint of the writer's professional interest. And we have already referred to the metaphor for " shrinking back," namely " shortening sail," which may —indirectly—betray the same interest.

It is evident that one main authority lies behind the letter (xi. 32, xiii. 19, 22, 23, *cf*. x. 24, 38). And if we are to choose between the two, it is no objection to our attributing the letter mainly to Priscilla to say that there are few, if any, traces of a woman's hand in it. Even these are perhaps not lacking. The writer is deeply interested in facts concerning parenthood and childhood (v. 12f., vii. 3, xi. 11f., xi. 23f., 28, 32, xii. 7f., etc.). Many of these would be equally appropriate from the pen of a man, but a certain pathos attaches to some of them. Melchisedec is described as "without father, without mother." It is not usual to describe Sarah's motherhood as an act of faith. The tenderness of the reason given for the hiding of the infant Moses by his parents is striking—" because they saw he was a beautiful child." So also is the description of Moses' act of faith—" he refused to be called the son of Pharoah's daughter." And the pathetic sacrifice of Jephthah is also one which would appeal to a woman. Still more suggestive of a woman's hand among the catalogue of faith's achievements is this reference: "Women received their dead raised to life again" (xi. 35). Even the omission of Deborah and Jael from among the heroines of faith, may have its own significance. The barbarous nature of their deeds may not have appealed to a womanly mind. Rendel Harris would

detect a woman's hand in one of the closing remarks :
" I have written a letter unto you *in few words* "
(xiii. 22). Interesting though the letter be, it can
hardly be termed brief ! And when in addition
to all these things, we remind ourselves once again
of the suspicious fact of the suppression of the writer's
name, the suggestion that it was Priscilla's hand that
wrote it, begins to appeal to us with a special strength.
It seems the best and the likeliest reason that can be
offered for the early reticence about the authorship.
The silence of women in matters of religion came
early, through the influence of Paul, to be regarded
as a dogmatic rule in the Church. And when
Clement of Rome wrote to Corinth quoting more
than once this letter as authoritative, he was writing
to the very church to which Paul had given his
strict injunctions about the place of women in the
Ecclesia. The authorship could not have been
forgotten in Rome at this very early date (95 A.D.).
Was it because the author was a woman, that he is
dumb ?

One more point remains to be considered. It was
Luther who first made the plausible conjecture that
Apollos was the author. This would certainly
explain the influence of the Alexandrian philosophy
apparent in the letter. But if Apollos were writing
to the church and the city where he first learned
Christ in all His fulness, it would be *to* Ephesus (vid. p.
168). And he could not have written in the tone of
authority and rebuke which is characteristic of this
letter, to Ephesus where he himself had blundered
through ignorance at the beginning. The likelihood, however, is that the letter was written *from*
Ephesus, since Timothy is mentioned as a colleague.
Moreover, Apollos was away from Ephesus before

the days of the riots there. He had really no church to which he could write, calling to mind the sufferings which he had endured with them immediately after their illumination. He might have written to Alexandria, where he received the first dim beginnings of his new faith ; but Timothy, whose projected visit the writer mentions as a matter of deep interest to the recipients of the letter, was not known in Alexandria. He was known in Rome, but Apollos apparently had had no intercourse with Rome.

But think for a moment of Apollos' story. He had come from Alexandria, fresh from the school of Philo, the adherent of a group of followers of the Baptiser, who still carried on the prophet's reformation propaganda there. He can hardly be called a Christian at this stage of his career. He was thoroughly cognisant no doubt of the Baptiser's teaching, and he and his sect were still full of the expectation of the imminent advent of the Messiah. The theme of John's message had been " Prepare ye the way of the Lord," and Luke tells us that this eloquent man, mighty in the scriptures, spoke in the synagogue at Ephesus on this theme—" the way of the Lord," knowing, he adds, only the baptism of John. It was Priscilla and Aquila who were the means of leading him to the light. And think of what happened afterwards when Paul arrived in the city. He found about a dozen converts of Apollos to this "way" of John. They had not so much as heard whether there was any Holy Spirit. They had only been baptised into John's baptism. And Paul first baptised them, and then, with the laying on of his hands, the Holy Spirit came upon them. Is there no echo of this very incident in this letter to the Hebrews ? " Therefore leaving the elementary parts of the doctrine of Christ behind, let us go on to what belongs to the initiates, instead of laying the foundation over again with repentance from dead works, with faith in God, with *instruction about baptisms and the laying on of hands. . . .*" (*cf.* Acts xix. 1-7 with Heb. vi. 1f.). Why, it is evident that it was precisely in these elementary things of the Christian faith that Apollos had been lacking. He also had need to be instructed. Does there not arise here the strong impression that this letter is just the deliberate and finished committal to writing of the teachings and discussions which Priscilla and Aquila had had with Apollos ? The whole line of the argument is just such as might be used with a learned Jew to show him how the new faith in its depth and wonder was the completion of the old. The idea of writing the letter in fact may have occurred to them through these discussions. This would help to explain the homiletic form, to some extent. The evidence all points to these two as the authors. (The story referred to in Acts (xviii. 24-xix. 7) probably came to Luke from them).

But we have already noted that certain features of the letter imply that one mind is mainly responsible for it. It is no disparagement of Aquila to suggest it was his wife. The lady seems to have been a Roman, high-born and well-educated, but in all probability she had become a proselyte of the Gate when she met Aquila and found her affinity in him. So deeply absorbed had she become in her new faith that it was quite natural for her to marry a Jew. The synagogue to which she had been attached in Rome may have had members who had

been influenced by the Alexandrian philosophy.
But surely, without that, her quick, earnest, enquiring
mind would have absorbed the main truths of
it readily enough in her discussions with Apollos.
Certainly Luke does not hesitate to say that she
had a share in persuading him to pass beyond the
faith of the Baptiser. The letter betrays no more
than just this amount of acquaintance with that
philosophy. And her chief glory was that she had
learned Christ. *Qui Jesum Christum novit*, says
Bengel, *potentes in scriptura docere potest*.

CHAPTER IX

A Page of Names

I

ROME was the political and social centre of the world when the religion of Christ began to make its way. Rome still claims to be the centre of the Christian world. It believes that its claim is founded in history ; that the Pope sits in St. Peter's chair, and to him alone has been bequeathed through Apostolic succession, the power of the keys.

" Thou art Peter," Jesus said to Simon the fisherman, " and on this rock will I build my church, and the gates of Hades shall not prevail against it." And the Roman Catholic Church maintains that Peter founded the Church in Rome, and was its first bishop. *They*, therefore, are the only real representatives of the primitive Church ; and, as such, they alone have the authority to dispense eternal life and death.

This tremendous claim raises the question of the origin of the Church in Rome to the status of a challenge. Can the story of the obscure beginnings of this Church be told ? Can we discover it from the pages of the New Testament ?

If our quest were a doctrinal one, we should deny that Christ deliberately set apart *Peter* as the foundation-stone of His Church. We do not believe that He meant that through this man, set apart as the first channel of Divine Grace, the entire stream was to flow down to the priesthood that historically descended from him, and through no other channel whatsoever. At the opposite extreme stands the view that Peter's confession : "Thou art the Christ, the Son of the living God," was the rock on which Christ meant to found His Church. But it was not this Creed, this definite form of words, that had appealed to Christ. And in point of fact it has not been made the one Confession of the Church of Christ in history. Not on Peter the man, not on the rough, impulsive, wavering fisherman ; nor yet on his soaring confession did Christ found His Church. But on what Peter had become at that moment—a believing soul uttering the adoration of faith—on that was the foundation laid. Peter is the type of all believing souls who confess. And wherever we find believing souls making united acknowledgment of the Lordship of Jesus—there we have the Church.

But our quest is rather for the evidence of history concerning this tremendous claim of the Church of Rome. And the track is hard to follow, for there are many gaps, many points where it is quite overgrown. And first there is a thicket of groundless assertion to cut through, ere we get into the neighbourhood of the true way. The claim of the Roman Church is that it was through Peter that the light of the new faith first sprang to birth in Rome. He came to Rome in the year 42 A.D., they say, was the first to preach Christ there, was the founder of the Church, and remained its bishop for a continuous period of twenty-five years thereafter.

The opportunity provided by the New Testament for such a tradition is meagre in the extreme. We read in the book of Acts that after Peter had escaped from prison, and had reported himself to his friends in the house of the Upper Room, "he went to *another place*." This vague "other place," it is maintained, was Rome (Acts xii. 17).

But we turn over a few pages of the book of the Acts, and on the page that records the dispute between Jewish and Gentile Christians, when the matter is referred to the Apostles and elders at the head of the Church in Jerusalem, we find that it is Peter who first stands up to give the weight of his authority on the side of the Gentiles. And this is only ten years after the date when he is supposed to have gone to Rome. It would seem that he had only separated himself from the Church in Jerusalem during the brief period while his life was in danger, and, so far from being absent from Palestine twenty-five years, he may on this occasion never even have crossed its frontier. When Paul writes his letter to Galatia, he knows of no residence of Peter outside Palestine, except in Antioch. And when he writes later to Rome, and speaks of his longing to visit the eternal city, he says it is " by way of refreshing your memory I have written to you somewhat boldly, in virtue of my Divine commission as a minister of Christ Jesus to the Gentiles," and "I have made it my ambition always to preach the Gospel only in places where there had been no mention of Christ's name, for fear I should be building on another man's foundation." And he explains that it was because he had found so many openings elsewhere in the East, that he had been prevented again and again from coming to them (Rom. xv. 15f 20f.). Surely if that means anything it means that Paul was certain that neither Peter nor any of the other Apostles had preached in Rome. And this letter was written seven years after that

conference in Jerusalem—seventeen years after the
date which the Church of Rome believes to mark
the commencement of Peter's long ministry in that
city. And in the account of Paul's arrival in Rome
—three years later still—it is related that he found
the Jews there expressing only the haziest notion
of what had been going on in the East. No one had
written or told them of Paul and his doings. No
authoritative person had given them any account of
Christianity ; and though they had their suspicions
of this sect that was everywhere spoken against,
they were willing to give Paul a hearing that they
might judge at first hand (Acts xxviii. 17-23).
Twenty years after the date of Peter's supposed
arrival in Rome ! True, towards the end of the
second century we begin to hear of the Church in
Rome having been " founded and constituted by
the two very glorious Apostles Peter and Paul."
But Irenaeus is speaking loosely or under a mis-
apprehension. Clement of Rome, writing about
the middle of the second century, while he speaks
of the two as known witnesses to the truth, does
not claim them as founders of the church in the
eternal city. And Ignatius writing about the same
time, states the truth accurately when he says that
Peter and Paul were known in Rome, and their
influence was recognised there, but not that they
were founders. When Paul writes his letter to
Philippi, possibly about the end of his second year's
imprisonment in Rome, there is still no sign that
Peter had come. The earliest tradition to which
any probability attaches is that recorded in Eusebius'
History of the Church, which represents Peter and
Paul together in Rome and together suffering
martyrdom during the Neronian persecution.

We may take it as certain, therefore, that Christianity had come to Rome long before either Peter or Paul had visited it. When Paul landed at Puteoli, he " found brethren " there, and a week later he was met on the way up to the imperial city by other brethren (presumably from the capital) at Appii Forum and " Three Taverns " (Acts xxviii. 14f.). Paul's letter to Rome, sent to herald his coming, was addressed to Christians who were already there, and we gather from the letter that they already had the sacrament of Baptism, and were in the habit of celebrating the Lord's Supper, even if they had not as yet been organised into one Church.

How then, did the Cross come to Rome ? How much do we know about these first Roman Christians ? Let us open the last page of Paul's letter to the Roman Church. It is a page of names. Has it any story to tell ?

II

It is the very general opinion of recent criticism that this is not a bit of the letter to Rome at all. It is a loose page of a letter to Ephesus, which has somehow found its way into this Roman letter or got tacked on to the end of it. The ascription which closes the chapter is placed by some MSS. at the end of the fourteenth chapter, as though the letter ended there at one time. But it is not characteristically Pauline, and may have been a liturgical addition by a later hand when the letter came to be read in Christian churches. It is not impossible that Paul may have used the letter as an encyclical, after it had fulfilled its first purpose as a communication to Rome, and in doing so may have omitted the fifteenth chapter and the long list of greetings

(sixteenth) when he sent it elsewhere. There are
three benedictions, however, which seem puzzling
(xv. 33, xvi. 20, and xvi. 24). But the last is
probably an interpolation. So that we are left
with two. And this gives us little ground for
supposing that the letter is not a unity. Often
when long letters are sent, they are enclosed in a
letter of personalities, which forms a kind of
envelope ; or a long document is sent in a covering
letter, as we may suppose the Fourth Gospel to have
been sent with the first Epistle of John as a preface
or afterword. It may be so here. The letter to
Rome may have been finished for some time before
an opportunity occurred for sending it. And when
Phoebe passed through Corinth on her way to Rome,
the Apostle may have seized the opportunity, and
given her this commendatory letter, with the special
greetings. There is nothing in these external
peculiarities that forbids us ascribing this chapter
to Paul when he first sent this whole letter to the
community in Rome. And unless we find insuperable difficulties in the chapter itself, we have no real
reason before us, requiring us to say it is another
letter or part of another letter altogether. Four
reasons are adduced for the view that it is a letter
to Ephesus : (1) The greeting to Priscilla and Aquila,
(2) the greeting to Epaenetus, the first-fruits of
Asia, (3) the fact that Paul knew about so many—
an unlikely familiarity with a church he had never
visited, (4) the special descriptions he attaches to
so many. None of these reasons are insurmountable.

And four preliminary general considerations
deserve to be mentioned by way of countering these:
(a) There are five or six distinctively Roman
names, Junias, Ampliatus, Urbanus, Rufus, Julia—

one of which at least—Junias—was borne by a Jew ; and of the thirteen or so Greek names, three or four at least, probably more, Andronicus, Apelles (Abel), etc., are the names of Jews. There were many Jews and Greeks in the imperial city, some of them traders, some slaves.

(*b*) Of the twenty-six Christians definitely named or designated (for two are unnamed), no less than fourteen bear names which have been found on sepulchral inscriptions of persons of Caesar's household who were contemporary with Paul, and nine or ten are Greek :—Urbanus, Rufus, Ampliatus, Julia, Junias, Stachys, Apelles, Tryphæna, Tryphosa, Hermes, Hermas, Patrobas, Philologus, Nereus.

(*c*) Again, of the twenty-six it is only twelve with whom it can be maintained that Paul claims personal acquaintance. And in the case of four of these, the personal acquaintance is at least doubtful.

(*d*) When it is remembered that Paul had heard all about the Christians in Rome from Priscilla and Aquila ; and further that there was a full and constant intercourse between the East (particularly Ephesus and Corinth) and the imperial city, a great deal of the wonder that Paul should have known so many is removed.

But now when we begin to study the names in detail, one question at once arises to the lips about all the special descriptions he attaches to them. Why is Paul at such pains to claim familiarity with, and to tell so much about so many of them ? It is quite out of the usual course in his letters. Why is it that he thus strains every nerve to recall all that he knows of these friends ? Is it at all likely that he would do so in writing to a congregation with whose members he had had long and intimate intercourse, and with whom he hoped to be in touch soon again ? Surely the psychological probabilities are all against that. It is far more likely that he is writing to a community with which he has had as yet little to do, and with which he wants to ingratiate himself by recalling every possible tie he knows of.

But why tarry over this general consideration ? Let us come to the details. The chapter begins : " Let me introduce our sister Phoebe, a deaconess of the church at Cenchreæ ; receive her in the Lord as saints should receive one another, and give her any help she may require. She has been a help herself to many people, including myself . . ." Phoebe may have tended Paul in sickness at Cenchreæ, on his way home from his second journey (Acts xviii. 18). It is quite unnecessary to suppose that because she belonged to Cenchreæ she was therefore sailing from Cenchreæ, and that accordingly her destination must be a port on the coast of Asia. Paul wrote his letter to Rome from Corinth, and if Phoebe were travelling to Rome she would naturally cross the isthmus to Corinth and sail from there. And of course she would call and say good-bye to the Christian friends in Corinth. Probably she would have some days to spend with them waiting a suitable vessel. Paul would gladly seize the occasion of Phoebe's journey as a providential opportunity for the sending of a letter as a preliminary to the fulfilling of the resolves he had made in this very town. Here all his longings Romewards had been stirred by the news of the coming of the Cross to Rome, which Aquila and Priscilla had related to him. Nay, his longings would have been all the keener at this moment, if these two friends were once more in Rome.

And notice how he proceeds. The introduction of Phoebe is soon over. She had her own errand and her own friends. A general introduction to the whole Christian community needed few words from him. " Salute Prisca and Aquila, my fellow-workers in Christ Jesus, who have risked their lives for me ; I thank them and not only I but all the Gentile Churches as well." These are the words that have given the critics greatest pause in assigning this chapter to the letter to Rome.

Is it not the case that when Paul joined these two people in Corinth, they were exiles, recently expelled from Rome ? And when we find him leaving their company at length, they are settling down in Ephesus. Six years have passed since then. Are they now, at the date of this letter, back in Rome ? Some eight years later, when Paul writes from Rome to Timothy, bishop of *Ephesus*, he sends greetings to Prisca and Aquila. Had they never left Ephesus ? And must we give up the view that this chapter is part of the letter to Rome ? They had been driven out from Rome as disturbers of the peace.—True, but the edict of Claudius had never been fully carried out ; there were too many Jews in Rome to make it practicable. In fact it had very soon fallen into abeyance. Why, Paul's letter to Rome was sent to a community in part *Jewish*-Christian, and later, when he came to Rome, the first thing he did was to invite the *synagogue* to a conference. And surely Prisca and Aquila would have many a tie calling them back to the city where their home had been, and where many of their first Christian associates and friends still lived. " My fellow-workers in Christ " Paul calls them ; but there was no reason why he should say that to Ephesian Christians.

They all knew how intimately these two had been associated with Paul in the work there. But if this is a genuine bit of the letter to Rome, he would have every reason to say it. He is anxious to give as many reasons as he can for his desire to visit Rome ; and he is saying in effect, " I have old friends and fellow-workers among you." And " they risked their necks for my sake." Only in Ephesus or Corinth could this incident have occurred. Not Corinth, surely. There had been no need of any intervention there. Gallio, the strictly constitutional Roman, refused to interfere in the religious controversy, and drove Paul's accusers from the judgment-seat. But would there be any need to remind the Ephesians of something that had occurred in their midst so recently ? And surely the very fact that Prisca and Aquila had incurred danger in Ephesus would be an urgent reason why they should leave the city—for a time at least. Whither would they go, if not to their old home in Rome, where all their longings were ? And Paul, writing to Roman Christians who were ignorant of it all, would be proud to tell what these two friends of his had done for him. " I and all the Gentile Churches send our grateful thanks to them." Surely that word is not at all appropriate if Paul is writing from a town in the midst of the Greek Churches to a town in the midst of the Asiatic Christians. " All the Gentile Churches " means all the Churches in Greece and Asia. The phrase is only appropriate if he is writing from the midst of these Gentile Churches to some distant community of Christians whom he has never seen ; and all the more appropriate if that community is prominently Jewish-Christian. . . . " Also salute the Church that meets in their house." Prisca and Aquila did have a congregation in their house when they first settled at Ephesus (1 Cor. xvi. 19), though not in the very early days of the Gospel there (Acts xviii. 19, 26, xix. 8, 9). But this very fact throws light on the present problem. For when Paul writes—years after this letter to Rome—to the bishop of Ephesus, and sends greetings to these old friends of his, he makes no mention of a church in their house ; in fact immediately after the mention of their names he adds " and the household of Onesiphorus," indicating thereby that it was in *his* house Prisca and Aquila were now in the habit of worshipping. The implication surely is that the former congregation in their house in Ephesus had been broken up for some reason, and not, so far, resumed. What more likely reason can be suggested than that they had been absent for a prolonged period, and had possibly only recently returned when Paul wrote to Timothy (2 Tim. iv. 19, *vid. sup.* p. 177f.) ?

But would they have a church in Rome on their return thither, seeing that they had been absent from the place so long ? They had evidently been leaders in the great Christian movement that had flamed up in the Ghetto in Rome in the year 49 A.D. (Acts xviii. 2). But they had been driven from Rome soon after this "enlightenment." There had been no time then to consolidate a congregation in their house from among the first-fruits of the revival. If the letter to the " Hebrews " was written by these two, must we not postulate some time of sojourn in Rome between the date of their expulsion and the writing of the letter ? For this letter was directed to a congregation that had been sufficiently strong to maintain its identity during the years of their subsequent absence. Surely they did pay a prolonged visit to Rome some time after their expulsion. And if they had resumed their old life in Rome, what more natural than to suppose that they had once more taken their places as leaders of such a congregation? An authority of this kind is clearly presupposed by the letter to the "Hebrews."

And to whom would Paul send his earliest greetings, if not to his old friends who had first told him the story of the coming of the Cross to Rome? It would be the congregation that met in their house that he would mainly have in mind when he wrote his letter. It is addressed to a prominently Jewish-Christian community, even if the majority were Gentiles.

There is an old church still standing on the Aventine in Rome, which from the fourth to the eighth century was known as the church of St. Prisca. After this it was given the *Titulus Aquilae et Priscae*. The husband's name is added and put first. Does it not mark the forcefulness of the lady's personality that it is she alone who is first canonised? It strengthens the case for thinking that Prisca was mainly responsible for "Hebrews" to note here again the tendency to depreciate the place and work of women in the Church, a tendency which was probably the reason for the suppression of the author's name in the case of this letter. But it is surely very significant also that this old church is sometimes called *Domus Aquilae et Priscae*. The *house!* Perhaps the church is even built on the original site of this place of early Christian gathering—the most important site in short in the early history of the Church in Europe.

III

Already the mists seem lifted somewhat from the story of the Cross in Rome. Let us further pursue this list of names. " Salute my beloved Epænetus, the first in Asia to be reaped for Christ." There is nothing intrinsically improbable in conjecturing that in these days of constant intercourse between Asia and the centre of the Empire, this Asiatic should have some time emigrated to Rome. But the probabilities strengthen when we begin to consider the case of Epænetus. " The first in Asia to be reaped for Christ " was surely won to Christianity on the occasion of Paul's first brief visit to Ephesus with Prisca and Aquila (Acts xviii. 19). For a time the cause hung fire in Ephesus—till the meteoric appearance of Apollos. Would not Prisca and Aquila befriend the lonely convert ? Perhaps, suffering ostracism for his faith, he was employed by Aquila in the tentmaking, and became their devoted friend. Is it unnatural to suppose that when the two were forced to leave the town, he would travel with them to Rome ? Why describe him as the first to be won in Asia, if this page of names was directed to Ephesus. Most Christians there would know ; but in Rome the fact would be full of fresh interest. In view of all this it is somewhat exciting to discover that among the sepulchral inscriptions of this date found in Rome, there is one—to Epænetus, an Ephesian !

" Salute Mary, who has toiled hard for us," the letter goes on. " You," is no doubt a better attested reading than " us." Nevertheless, copyists may have changed it because of the difficulty in Paul's saying " us," when the person spoken of was in Rome.

A Page of Names

And can we not find a significance in this reference to some one who, on the received reading, had " slaved " for Paul ? " Slaved " is undoubtedly the import of the word. And since her service for Paul must have been recent, she must have recently settled in Rome. It can hardly be John Mark's mother. Mark did not come to Rome till later. Yet there is no further designation of this bearer of a very common name. But if we conjecture she was a Christian slave in the household of Prisca and Aquila, the vagueness at once disappears. Prisca, Aquila, Epænetus and Mary are all named together, and there is nothing unlikely in the conjecture that they form a single household. Paul, with his delicate Christian courtesy, remembers how Mary toiled for him when he was an inmate of this household in Corinth and Ephesus. These four names would thus account for half the number of those with whom it can confidently be said that Paul here claims acquaintance.

Following upon these we might expect the names of some of the Jewish Christians who belonged to this congregation in Prisca's house. " Salute Adronicus and Junias, fellow-countrymen and fellow-prisoners of mine ; they are men of note among the Apostles, and they have been in Christ longer than I have." Paul at once confirms our expectation here, informing us that these were Jews ; for when he speaks of kinsmen he means race-relations not blood-relations. But they were probably not residents in Palestine, for they bear Greek and Roman names ; Jews of the Dispersion most likely. Early discipleship was an honourable distinction in the primitive Church. Perhaps they were among the crowd from all parts of the Empire who were won for Christ in Jerusalem on the day of Pentecost. The fact that they were disciples before Paul, would take us back to those days, if not even further still. " Strangers of Rome " were in that Pentecost crowd. If the phrase " among the Apostles " means " in the number of the apostles," their following of Jesus would go further back still—back to the days when He was alive. But it may only mean that they were recognised by the Apostles as men of outstanding faith. The phrase " fellow-prisoners of mine " does not necessarily mean that they were imprisoned along with Paul. Indeed it is difficult to imagine where they could have shared such an imprisonment with him. It could not have been in Philippi, for they were not in the company of Paul in that town; nor yet in Ephesus, for the historian expressly indicates that Paul was preserved by his friends from rough treatment there (Acts xix. 29ff.) ; nor yet in Corinth either, for his treatment there can hardly be called imprisonment. In short, the only recorded imprisonment up to this time was one which they almost certainly did not share—in Philippi ; and if it had been in Ephesus, it would have been superfluous to have mentioned the fact, if this page was part of a letter to Ephesus. But if the phrase means that they had shared a similar fate, though in another place, the way opens up for an interesting surmisal. If we are right about the origin and destination of the letter to the " Hebrews," Christianity began in Rome through the preaching of some that had heard the Lord (Heb. ii. 3). And as a result of the commotion which followed the " illumination " there, some of the leaders of the new movement, it would seem, were put under restraint (Heb. x. 34).

A Page of Names

Was it then partly through the preaching of Andronicus and Junias that the congregation of Jewish
Christians took origin in Prisca's house ? To these
Jews, freed-men perhaps of Greek and Roman
masters, or to such as these, the Church in Rome
owes its birth. To the activity of such as these the
edict of Claudius was due. In the words of Suetonius,
" he expelled the Jews who were persistently rioting,
a certain *Chrestus* being the moving spirit."

The names which immediately follow : Ampliatus,
Urbanus, Stachys, Apelles, may also have been
leaders in this Jewish-Christian congregation. We
do not know enough to say that they were all Jews :
two are Latin, two are Greek names. But Apelles
looks like a Græcised form of the Hebrew name
" Abel," and Ampliatus, " my beloved in the Lord,"
and Stachys, " my beloved," would seem, as these
phrases suggest, to have been known to
Paul ; may indeed have been converts—or fellow-
workers. Urbanus is described as the latter. " My
fellow-worker in Christ " is Paul's commonest
description of active Christians ; and here the phrase
is " *our* fellow-worker." The word may include
Prisca and Aquila ; fellow-workers with these,
they would be fellow-workers with Paul also. The
names Ampliatus and Urbanus are found in similar
juxtaposition in a list of imperial freedmen on a
Roman tomb-inscription of date 115 A.D. Almost
more suggestive still is the appearance of the name
Ampliatus on the catacomb of Domitilla, a high-
born Roman lady who became a Christian towards
the end of the first century. It seems probable
that a person of this name " was conspicuous in the
earliest Roman Church, and may have been the means
of introducing Christianity to a great Roman house."

Stachys and Apelles are Greek names, and appear as slave-names on sepulchral inscriptions of the imperial household. Perhaps they were leading members, not of Prisca's congregation, but of the little community of Christians which Paul is about to mention.

For we must hasten now to say that the earliest Christians in Rome were not all Jews. A careful reading of Paul's letter to Rome convinces us that there were Gentiles as well as Jews, perhaps more Gentiles than Jews, among the first Christians of Rome. And the page of names continues, "Salute them of the household of Aristobulus." In other words, "Salute the Christian slaves in the retinue of Aristobulus." We seem to pass here quite definitely to another little house-church, whose members were associates in the same serfdom. And contemporary history tells us of a certain Aristobulus, who was grandson of Herod the Great. A friend and adherent of the Emperor Claudius, he apparently lived and died in a private station. Although he was probably dead by this time, and his slaves, no doubt, added to his friend the Emperor's household, they would still be known by the name of their former master. The identification of this group of Christians with the members of this slave-retinue who were Christians, has the highest degree of probability. It is no argument against this that Paul would have used the term 'Αριστοβουλίανοι if he were referring here to the slave-retinue of a man of that name. Apart from the fact that Paul is not always careful either with words or syntax, he could not well have used the word here, for he was not sending greetings to the entire slave-retinue of Aristobulus, but only, as the phrase correctly suggests, to the handful who had become Christian. There can be little doubt that this grandson of Herod, would have had Jewish slaves in his retinue. We have seen that "Apelles," who may be one of them, is probably a Græcised form of "Abel." But look further at the name that follows this greeting to them of the household of Aristobulus: "Salute Herodion, my kinsman." Does not the name indicate a member of the retinue of some prince of the dynasty of Herod? Perhaps he was born to Aristobulus by some Jewish slave-girl in his palace, and had received the name half in endearment, half in contempt—" Herodling," or "Little Herod." It would be like the tender Christian courtesy of Paul to call such an one " my kinsman." Fellowship in Christ blots out all marks of degradation and shame. Tradition has it that both Herodion and Olympas (later named) were beheaded at Rome when Peter was crucified.

But now another house-church comes into view. "Greet them that be of the household of Narcissus, which are in the Lord." The very form of the phrase—"those of the household of Narcissus—those in the Lord "—shows that Paul is conscious he is not addressing the entire household of Narcissus, and could not say Ναρκισσίανοι. Three or four years before the date of this letter, a well known freedman, Narcissus, a man of proverbial wealth, and exercising a powerful influence in the dynastic intrigues of the time, was put to death by Agrippina, on the accession of Nero to the imperial throne. His slaves were doubtless added to the imperial retinue. He was not a Christian any more than Aristobulus. It is difficult for those who believe this to be a fragment of a letter to Ephesus to parry the strong

probability that these are the households referred
to here. No such names can be identified as
belonging to Ephesus; indeed, not one person in
all the chapter, outside the household of Prisca,
can be claimed as ever belonging to that city. And
the strong probability that these households—parts
of Cæsar's retinue—are the households referred to
here, is greatly heightened by a word in Paul's letter
from Rome to the Church at Philippi; "All God's
people here salute you, especially they who are of
Cæsar's household" (Phil. iv. 22). It is clear
that from the very outset Christianity had gained
a footing among the imperial slaves: so many of
the names here given are common among slaves.
That they would suffer persecution for their faith
is a matter of course. Apelles is here described as
"that tried Christian," a Jewish slave probably, who,
because of his prominence during the commotions
of the days of the illumination (Heb. x. 32), had
suffered for his adherence to the new faith. These
little house-churches must have met furtively, in
the seclusion of the palace grounds, among the
catacombs, or in other secret places; and in constant
fear of detection. Tryphaena and Tryphosa, the
ladies "dainty" and "delicate" (or "disdain"),
who bear Greek names, may have belonged to this
Christian community. Paul plays upon their names
when he commends them for the way in which they
do their hard drudgery work "in the Lord." In
all probability they were twin sisters. For
similar-sounding names frequently indicated this
in ancient times. And Persis he knows of; probably
Prisca and Aquila had told him with what affection
she was regarded by the first Christians in Rome.
"The beloved," he calls her. She was an aged

saint, it would seem, for he speaks as if the days of her hard drudgery were over. "She *has* toiled strenuously in the Lord." Perhaps it means that she, too, had been an active Christian propagandist in the days of the enlightenment. The delicacy of Paul's reference is apparent here. Persis is " *the* beloved," not " my," nor " our " beloved, as in the case of Ampliatus and Stachys. And he is chivalrous too : it is of women only he uses the word for strenuous toil.

IV

The reference which follows is a deeply interesting one. It is perhaps the most intimate reference in the chapter, and at first sight it would seem to be all against the claim of this chapter to be part of the letter to Rome. " Salute Rufus, one of the Lord's chosen ; also his mother, who has been a mother to me."

But the name leads us out along another strand of the romance of the Cross, so wonderful that we are fain to say it ought to be true. The fact that the coming of the Cross to Rome did cause something like a little Pentecost down in the Ghetto seems to suggest that it was a breath of the Spirit, borne from the rushing, mighty wind of the Jerusalem awakening, that lit the sacred fire in Rome. Many of these first converts on the streets of the Holy City had been influenced, doubtless, by Jesus in the days of His flesh. And some of them were strangers from " Rome " (Acts ii. 10). Was the Roman centurion from Capernaum there, or that other centurion who with a deep stirring of the spirit watched Him die ? And does the name " Rufus " suggest nothing to our minds ? " Chosen in the

Lord," Paul calls him, as if his singling out for Christ's service had almost been due to an act of our Lord Himself. Let us assume that he belonged to the Roman Christians, and see whither the facts will carry us. He was a well-known Christian in this community. Is there any mention of him elsewhere in the New Testament ? In the Gospel of Mark we are told of a man who was "the father of Alexander and Rufus." Why does Mark insert these names without further comment ? Obviously because they were well-known Christians in the community in whose midst Mark wrote his Gospel. This was in Rome, and only a few years subsequent to the time of this letter of Paul's. Two outstanding Christians of the same name, contemporaries in the same community, must have been further distinguished in the documents of the time. It is practically certain that the Rufus mentioned by Paul and by Mark is one and the same person. "They took Jesus away to crucify Him," says Mark, " and they forced Simon a Cyrenian, who was passing on his way from the country (the father of Alexander and Rufus) to carry His cross " (Mark xv. 21). Striking indeed is the story which these facts reveal.

Simon of Cyrene, the swarthy proselyte from the far-off colony in Northern Africa, had come a pilgrim to this memorable Passover in Jerusalem. Making the most of his religious opportunities, he was probably coming in from the camping ground outside the city to pay his morning vows in the Temple. Suddenly a rabble burst from the Damascus gate. He heard the loud cries " Crucify, crucify." He saw the glitter of the Roman spears ; and in the midst, three figures dragging the ghastly gibbets on which they were about to be hung. Then the crowd stopped. For a moment the angry cries were silent, and the wailing of women fell on his ears. He had stood aside to let the sickening sight go past; but on the impulse he stepped again into the roadway to learn the cause of the delay. One of the victims, a pale, worn, bleeding Figure, had stumbled and fallen beneath the heavy beam that now pinned Him to the earth. And as he watched the Roman soldiers lifting it off the Man, he was touched on the shoulder by a haughty Roman spear. It was the signal of impressment. Vain to protest against the imperial majesty of Rome! Ere he was well aware what had happened, he was on the way to the hill of punishment, bearing— Another's cross. As this unwilling actor in a deed of unspeakable horror and shame felt the loathsome burden on his shoulder, his whole frame must have quivered with dread and repulsion. Was he the victim of a dream unsightly, or was it his own cross he was carrying? And then he looked at that torn and fainting Figure, dragged—almost borne—along by the rough soldiers, in a state of exhaustion and collapse; and he remembered. Yonder was the criminal, whoever He was; and *he* was carrying His burden! Cruel irony of fate to be made the substitute for a stranger who was nothing to him, whom he had never seen before, whose very crime he was ignorant of! So he toiled up the hillside with sense of wrong and outrage burning in his breast. When he reached the fatal spot he laid the Cross down, no doubt, with a right good will, and hurried away without waiting for a single word of recognition for his help. Let others wait to see the cruel nails battered through the trembling flesh—to see the writhing figures hoisted on the hill, as with a jarring

Gospel influence that reached the capital of the Empire, and helped to plant the Cross in Cæsar's household, where it grew and grew until the great Cæsar himself, ruler of the then civilised world some three hundred years after Calvary, had to bow his head and say, " Galilean, thou hast conquered."

Very likely it was on the streets of Jerusalem, at Pentecost, when the crowds were listening to Peter, Cyrenians amongst them, that Simon heard at length the story of the Nazarene whose Cross he bore. And the light broke on his path. When others gloried in the amazing career, calling Jesus " Son of God," perhaps when he heard Paul declaring in his passionate way that the Cross of Christ was all his boast, Simon was able proudly to say : " I carried it for Him ; I was permitted to share His suffering ; that was my golden morning, when I was called from all my own hopes and plans to take up the burden of Another ; and I did not let it drop."

V

So even this intimate reference in the letter does not debar us from thinking that Rome was the destination of this page. It rather tends to strengthen the proof, and gives us a vivid and entrancing story of one of the ways in which the Cross reached the centre of the ancient world. But our page of names is not yet exhausted.

" Salute Asyncritus, Phlegon, Hermes, Patrobas, Hermas and the brethren that are with them." These are all men's names ; and most, if not all of them, have been found on sepulchral inscriptions of the imperial household. They are all Greek names, and this suggests that they were compatriots, possibly members of the same slave-retinue, and for that reason associated in a congregation by themselves. The phrase " the brethren that are with them " indicates that Paul is mentioning only the most prominent, possibly the senior Christians, " the first nucleus, the leading individuals " of the congregation. Asyncritus, who is named first, may have been at their head. Pseudo-Dorotheus asserts that Patrobas—the name of a freedman contemporary of Nero—became bishop of Puteoli. If Hermas is the author of the ancient " Pilgrim's Progress " which bears his name—*The Shepherd of Hermas*—he had been a slave, sold to a certain Rhoda in Rome. He describes himself as " patient and good-tempered, and always smiling," " full of all simplicity and great guilelessness." After a period of worldliness and sharp practice in business, as a freedman, he lost his wealth through the misdeeds of his ill-trained family. Saddled with a sharp-tongued wife, dull-witted himself and filled with an endless curiosity, he at length became " useful and profitable unto life." (He may have seen Paul's letter about Onesimus— " useful," who became useless, and was made " profitable "—and been comforted by this prodigal's story.) He seems to have been one of those who felt keenly the rebuke and the reproach of the writer of the Epistle to the Hebrews in Rome ; and to have been greatly exercised by that stern word which speaks of the impossibility of repentance for post-baptismal sins (Heb. vi. 4, xii. 17). He writes to mitigate the severity of the word, and to make an earnest call to repentance. The story is alluring, although the fragment of Muratori forbids the identification with Paul's Hermas.

Yet a fifth little Christian community is mentioned

14

here. " Salute Philologus and Julia, Nereus and his
sister, and Olympas, and all the saints that are with
them." Philologus the Greek, and Julia the Roman
are probably man and wife, the hosts of this little
house-church. Nereus and his sister— Nereis ?—
and Olympas may be his family. Nereus is said
to have been a *diaconus* of the Christian Princess
Domitilla. Among the names of the inscriptions
is that of Domitia Nereis, wife of an imperial freedman. Lightfoot cites the case of a Claudia Aug. L.
Nereis, related to a mother and daughter Tryphaena.
A tradition of the *Hypomnema of Peter and Paul*
relates that Olympas was beheaded along with
Herodion, when Peter was crucified.

So by tracing out the connections of these names
on this New Testament page, we have learned much
about these five groups or churches of the earliest
Christians in Rome—something of the origin of
Christianity in the Eternal City, and some dim
glimpses of their experience as Christians. Ten at
least of these names—Stachys, Apelles, Tryphaena,
Tryphosa, Hermes, Hermas, Patrobas, Philologus,
Julia, Nereus, are found as names of persons connected with Cæsar's household and contemporary
with Paul, on sepulchral inscriptions on the Appian
Way. Perhaps some of these Christians whom
Paul here names are among the victims who
were " worried by dogs, or crucified, or burned as
lights for the performances in Nero's gardens, with
Nero himself in a jockey's dress, mixing with the
crowd or driving in a chariot." For many were
buried on this Appian Way. So they passed— " My
beloved Stachys," "Apelles, that tried Christian,"
and the rest. There they rest in peace. Their
names are written in the Book of Life.

A Page of Names

VI

In his second letter to Timothy Paul adds a few more names to the list : " Eubulus greets you ; so do Pudens, Linus, Claudia, and all the brotherhood." Eubulus, a Roman Christian with a Greek name, may have been a slave or a Roman freedman ; he is otherwise quite unknown. One tradition has it that Prisca was the mother of Pudens ; another that Claudia was the mother of Linus. Since they are mentioned together here, Pudens and Claudia may be husband and wife, and Linus their son. Roman tradition makes Pudens a senator, and the host of Peter when he came to Rome. He is said to have suffered martyrdom along with Aristarchus and Trophimus and Paul. Irenæus and Eusebius both regard Linus as the first bishop of Rome after the Apostles. In the Syriac *Teaching of Simon Cephas*, it is said that he was a disciple of Peter, a deacon, whom the Apostle makes bishop in his stead ; and that it was he who took up the bodies of Peter and Paul by night and buried them. It has been suggested that he was bishop of Rome from 64 to 76 A.D., after which Clement succeeded him.

The evidence is flimsy for the tale with which we would close this chapter ; but it kindles a certain interest in us who inhabit these islands. The poet Martial had a friend called Pudens, a soldier and a contemporary of Paul. To him the poet casually imputes the foulest vices of heathenism. But he also tells us the name of his bride—Claudia Rufina ; and this lady was of British birth. In the year 1722, a fragmentary Roman inscription was found at Chichester, which records that a Roman soldier, Pudens, the husband of Claudia, presented the site for a temple to the British king Cogidubnus; and he built thereon a temple to Neptune. It was the Roman's gift to the barbarian king who had given him his daughter in marriage. It is a pardonable fancy that this may be the Pudens and Claudia who are here named as the intimates of Paul! For there was a Claudia, daughter of a British king who came to Rome in the train of Pomponia, wife of Aulus Plautus, the Roman commander in Britain. Were she and her husband won for Christ by the Apostle? Pudens may have come in contact with Paul, possibly through his having charge of the soldiers that guarded the aged prisoner. If the Apostle never realised his dream of visiting Spain and the islands beyond, one would like to think that the winning of these two may have been to him the first swallow, foretelling the coming of the Christian summer there.

CHAPTER X

The Second Son of Mary : James
the Just

THERE are two chapters of the early history of
Christianity that are very dim ; yet they are chapters
to which we often turn with fond and eager yearning,
seeking to gather up and blend together in one
harmonious picture every stray gleam of light we
can find. One is the story of the little company
in Jerusalem who formed the first Christian congregation. The other is the story of the Nazareth
family, the brothers and sisters of our Lord. If
we can recover a picture of the second brother,
James, from the scattered details with which history
provides us, the light from the torch thus kindled
may help to illumine both the paths which we
would fain explore.

The romance that lies hidden in the story of James
the brother of Jesus is the romance of a family
reconciliation that was a Divine reconciliation as
well. But before we can experience the full force
and tenderness of that moving story, we must first
endeavour to build, so far as it is permitted to us,
a picture of James the Christian. And in order
that we may do so, let us first gather together the
references in the New Testament that deal with this
phase of his career.

I

The most remarkable and the most crucial reference for the understanding of the story is a brief one in Paul's first letter to Corinth. He is speaking of the resurrection, and he says " Jesus was seen by Cephas, then by the twelve ; after that He was seen by over five hundred brothers all at one time, the majority of whom survive to this day though some have now fallen asleep ; *after that He was seen by James,* and then by all the Apostles, and finally He was seen by myself, by this so-called ' abortion ' of an apostle " (1 Cor. xv. 5-8). The James who is here said to have had a special experience of the risen Christ is clearly not one of the twelve disciples ; he is Jesus' brother.

This passage is the oldest evidence we have for the resurrection. It purports to give the appearances in their historical order. And we must look at it for a moment to ascertain the occasion of the appearance to James. We see Peter, who had denied his Lord, prostrate in an agony of longing for one more interview, in the awful days that followed the crucifixion, but baulked by the memory of the Cross, and the separating darkness and silence of the tomb. " He cannot be dead "—these were the words, half protest of frenzy, half question, that kept haunting his mind. It seemed only " that terrible tenacity of hopeless passion that will stand against the hosts of heaven, God's great array of facts." And yet the thought proved true. Somehow he became conscious of his Master's presence—a visitation from beyond the grave. And the great peace of assurance that he was forgiven fell on his anguished soul. The story of the interview is not told, but we see the reflection of it in that letter which was written long afterwards by him. He has hardly put pen to paper before he breaks out into the doxology, " Blessed be the God and Father of our Lord Jesus Christ! By His great mercy we have been born anew to a life of hope through the raising again from the dead of Jesus Christ, born to an unscathed, inviolate, unfading inheritance " (1 Peter i. 3f.). The reflection of it is seen, too, in that word which he spoke in Jerusalem at Pentecost: " It was not possible that He should be holden by death " (Acts ii. 24).

It was apparently in the garden of the sepulchre that the interview took place. And when he returned to the Upper Room the contagion of his conviction seized on the rest of the band, and then they too shared a similar experience. He had fulfilled his Lord's command to him, " When thou art converted, strengthen thy brethren " (Luke xxii. 32). Then followed a resuscitation of the faith of followers in Galilee through the disciples' testimony—an enthralling, glorious assurance of the living Presence and power of Jesus, taking possession of the lives of more than five hundred at once. *It was between this event and the Pentecostal Advent that James, the brother of the Lord, received his assurance that his Elder Brother was not dead.* The appearance to " all the apostles " was possibly the visitation at Pentecost. The eleven had returned to Jerusalem, and a company of about a hundred and twenty betook themselves to a time of prolonged, intense, and earnest prayer in the Upper Room, and the rushing breath of the Spirit on the day of Pentecost was the outcome. Paul has no hesitation in describing his experience on the road to Damascus as of a precisely similar nature

to that which the others had had; a sudden
illumination in which all the outside world became
immersed in glory, and in the light a heavenly
vision. He describes it elsewhere also, and without
any contradiction, as an inward vision. " It pleased
God to reveal His Son *in* me " (Gal. i. 16). " God
who commanded the light to shine out of darkness
is he who has shined in our hearts to give us the
light of the knowledge of the glory of God in the
face of Jesus Christ " (2 Cor. iv. 6).

Next in historic order of the references to James
is that in the Acts of the Apostles (i. 14). The list
of the eleven disciples is given, and then follow the
words ; " These all resorted with one mind to
earnest prayer, together with the women, with Mary
the mother of Jesus, and with His brothers."
Stirred to hope by James' experience and by
the disciples' recollection of His promise to return
with power, the sorrowing family had joined the
disciples to wait. This was in 29 A.D.

Nine years have passed and the scene is changed.
Paul has returned to Jerusalem after his Damascus
experience, and his three years' brooding in Arabia.
" He tried to join the disciples, but they were all
afraid of him, unable to believe he was really a
disciple. Barnabas, however, came to his assistance.
He brought him to the disciples and related to them
how he had seen the Lord upon the road, how the
Lord had spoken to him, and how he had fearlessly
taught in the name of Jesus at Damascus " (Acts
ix. 26ff.). Luke adds that " he then went in and out
among them at Jerusalem." But Luke has probably
over-emphasised this reconciliation with the
Apostles. Let us hear Paul's own witness : " After
three years I went up to Jerusalem to make the

acquaintance of Cephas. I stayed for fifteen days with him. I saw no other apostle, only James the brother of the Lord " (Gal. i. 18f.). From this word of Paul's we learn that Peter and James at this early date in the history of the Church somehow shared the pre-eminence in Jerusalem. Persecution, or perhaps special missions, had scattered most of the other leaders. This was in 38 A.D.

Once more the scene changes. James, the son of Zebedee, has been martyred by Herod. Peter has been imprisoned. It is the night of his escape. He comes to John Mark's mother's house, tells his story, and gives this injunction, as he prepares to go : " Report this to James and to the brothers (perhaps, *his brothers*)." It would seem from this that there were now at least two house-churches in Jerusalem, one in the Upper Room, and one the head of which was Jesus' brother James (Acts xii. 17). This was probably in 44 A.D.

The next glimpse we get of the man is on a dramatic amd highly critical occasion. The inevitable conflict had broken out between the Jewish Christians and the Gentile converts. The former had evidently not broken free from their old religion, in spite of the liberating deed of Stephen. They clung about the Temple and its worship. They regarded themselves rather as another sect within the ancient historic religion. And some of them had actually gone down and made trouble among Paul's converts. They had insisted that the Gentile believers must undergo the Jewish rite of circumcision, and keep the Jewish ceremonial Law about clean and unclean meats. Apparently the people who brought about this crisis were " some of the believers who belonged to the party of the Pharisees." Paul and Barnabas came up to Jerusalem and told their story, but these men interposed with their objections. A council was called, and after an acrimonious wrangle Peter rose. He was in favour of a liberal policy. No coercion of the Gentiles : that was his view, backed by his own experience in Cæsarea. Paul and Barnabas then followed in support. They repeated their testimony of the evident presence of the Spirit of God among the Gentiles, though none of the ancient rites and ceremonies were imposed. It was when they had finished that James made his appearance. " Men and brethren, hearken to me," he began. And at once it is evident that this man has attained to a position of peculiar authority and honour in the Church at Jerusalem. He corroborated Peter's attitude by a quotation from Amos. And then he added : " My judgment, therefore, is that we ought not to put unexpected difficulties in the way of those who are turning to God from among the Gentiles, but that we send them written instructions to abstain from the pollutions incurred in idolatry, from sexual vice, and from blood-outrage."

James was evidently president of the Council ; and his judgment became the finding of the house. Paul and Barnabas were sent away, along with two deputies bearing letters of liberation from all save the high ethical obligations which were binding upon all men. This was in 51 A.D. (Acts xv. 1-33).

It is well to set alongside this, Paul's excited—one might almost say angry and contemptuous—account of the meeting. In spite of this liberal decision of the meeting, the open sore was not healed. The Christian legalists continued to send emissaries into the Gentile field. They had met with some success among Paul's converts in Galatia. And Paul writes to rebuke his wavering followers, and to denounce these factious Jewish Christians. In emphatic and stormy language he declares that the Council had nothing to add to his Gospel. They did not dare to say that his message was deficient in any respect. On the contrary, he says, when those " so-called ' authorities ' (it makes no difference to me what their status was—God pays no regard to the external distinctions of man), . . . when James and Cephas and John, those reputed ' pillars ' of the church, perceived the mission which had been graciously entrusted to me, they gave Barnabas and me the right hand of fellowship. Our sphere was to be the Gentiles, theirs the circumcised " (Gal. ii. 6-9). Behind the sarcasm, we have here a testimony to the position of weighty authority James had taken in the Jerusalem Church. And so far as the decision of the Council shows, he is a man of tolerant views, a lover of Christian liberty, and above all of peace.

But the incident which Paul goes on to relate as happening subsequently does not leave such a fragrant impression of sweet reasonableness on the mind, as Luke's account of the Council does. Some time after this meeting, Peter paid a visit to Antioch, the head-quarters of the Gentile Christian Church. True to his speech in Council, true to his own experience, he did nor hesitate to lay his Jewish prejudices aside at first and sit at the same table with the Gentiles. Let Paul reveal what followed; only let it be premised that James may have had no part in the deputation, even though they professed to come from him : " But when Cephas came to Antioch I opposed him to his face. The man stood self-condemned. Before certain emissaries of James arrived, he ate along with Gentile Christians ; but when they arrived he began to draw back and hold aloof, because he was afraid of the circumcision party." "Certain emissaries from James," and "the circumcision party," are phrases which make it quite clear that in spite of the honour, the deference, and indeed the reverence which all sections of the Jerusalem Christians paid to James, Paul has the strong impression that he belonged to the party of believers who were strict and scrupulous Jews, still fulfilling all the Mosaic Law. Indeed, since some of the Pharisees had become Christian, and looked up to James for guidance, he must have shown not only a special reverence for the Law ; but so fulfilled it that men came to see in him an outstanding sanctity of character (Gal. ii. 11, 12).

The next glimpse that the Book of Acts gives of him would seem to bear this impression out. Paul has come up to Jerusalem again for the last time. And Luke writes : "The brothers welcomed us gladly on our arrival in Jerusalem. Next day we accompanied Paul to James ; all the presbyters were present." And after Paul had described what God had done among the Gentiles, "they said to him" (on account, they said, of the many thousands of believing Jews who had heard of his freedom with the Law), "Do as we bid you. We have four men here under a vow : associate yourself with them, purify yourself with them, pay their expenses, . . . then everyone will understand there is nothing in these stories. . . ." Here is a great church, thousands of Jew-believers, and James still at the head, indeed enjoying now unchallenged and unshared supremacy. It is a church which has contrived somehow to remain a sect of the ancient faith—obeying the Law, observing the old rites and ceremonies, joining in the Temple worship. Probably they called their own Christian meeting a synagogue. And the year of the Christian era at which we have now arrived is the year 58 A.D. —seven years after the Council (Acts xxi. 17-26).

Of the personal circumstances of James nothing can be affirmed with certainty from the pages of the New Testament. In his first letter to Corinth, Paul asks " Have we not a right to take with us on our journeys a Christian sister as our wife, like the rest of the Apostles, like the brothers of the Lord, like Cephas himself " (1 Cor. ix. 5) ? Evidently from this, some of Christ's brothers were married, though the word hardly justifies us in saying for certain that James was. James seems to have been accorded the title, certainly the rank of " Apostle " (Gal. i. 19). He first comes prominently on the scene of the Church's activity after the murder of James, the son of Zebedee, and he may have taken the place of his namesake in the number of the Twelve.

II

We have exhausted all the references to James outside the Gospels in the New Testament, save for *the letter* which bears his name. That James was the author is, of course, stoutly denied by many of the more " advanced " critics. The problem cannot be discussed here in full. But certain features of it must be briefly passed in review. The date cannot be very definitely determined. The phrase " transgressor of the law " (James ii. 11) occurs only once elsewhere in the New Testament

(Rom. ii. 25, *cf.* 27). Again the phrase " lusts that war in your members " (James iv. 1) looks like the echo of another word in the letter to Rome (vii. 23) ; and the sentiments about the trying of one's faith working patience (James i. 2-4) seem to reflect yet another thought of Paul's (Rom. v. 3-5). When James speaks of the keeper of the law who offends in one point being guilty of all, he is repeating another frequent conception of Paul's. And since a large part of his argument is taken up with the necessity of " works " as a demonstration of faith, it reads like a reply to an extreme interpretation of Paul's view. So that the epistle seems certainly later than that of Paul to Rome. It might be argued on the ot er hand that the letter of James was known to the writers of the epistles of John, the epistles to " the Hebrews " and to Timothy, and the first epistle of Peter. The corresponding sentiments in James seem more elementary, less guarded, and therefore more primitive. So that we may postulate some date prior to 65 A.D. The document is addressed " to the twelve tribes which are scattered abroad " (James i. 1). And if we cannot affirm that it comes straight from the pen of the brother of our Lord, we may at least suggest, for it seems an anthology of fragments of homilies, that it is a compilation of the sayings of James, made by a member of the Jerusalem Church, possibly after James' death, and some time prior to the fall of Jerusalem when the members of the Jewish Christian Church there were being scattered abroad. It would be cherished as a memorial of the man whom they had held in such honour in Jerusalem.

It is interesting to discover quaint and unusual turns of speech common to the letter and the speech of James and the decree of Council of A.D. 51 in Jerusalem. It is sometimes lightly assumed that Luke freely composed the speeches which are interspersed through his history. There is evidence that on more than one occasion he was at least working on a very circumstantial account of the speech. And here, when Luke says " Symeon " instead of his usual Simon, our expectation is at once aroused. And there are so many ἅπαξ λεγόμενα in these short passages, that we begin to feel Luke must be quoting a good many of James' words *verbatim*. The form " to greet " at the beginning of the letter of James, and of the letter of the decrees, is an unusual form in the New Testament. It occurs only one other time, where again it is probably an actual letter that is being copied by Luke (Acts xxiii. 26). The opening of James' speech at the council— " Brethren, hearken to me "—is paralleled in the Epistle (ii. 5). " Brethren," or " beloved brethren " is a favourite form of address in the Epistle; it is used some fifteen times. And the word " beloved "—used thrice in the Epistle (i. 16, 19, ii. 5)—is used only here, in the Letter of the Council (Acts xv. 25), and never elsewhere in Luke. The peculiar use of the word " to visit " (Jas. i. 27, *cf.* Acts xv. 14) seems a Hebraic expression in all the other instances where it is used by Luke—something said by a Jew, and not Luke's own. Similarly the expression " your souls " (Acts xv. 24) is a Hebraism (*cf.* Jas. i. 21, v. 20), as is the form of the word " Symeon." And the phrase " it seemed good to the Holy Spirit and to us," in the letter of the Council for which James was doubtless responsible, is—as we gather from the frequent similar usage in Acts—an Apostolic conception, a familiar point of view in the Jerusalem church.

The compound word meaning " to turn " (Acts xv. 19), used by James in his speech, is an unusual word for conversion in the New Testament, and it is used by James in the letter (v. 19f.). Similarly the expression " keep oneself from " (Acts xv. 29) is used in the letter (i. 27), and the Aramaic for τηρεῖν, διατηρεῖν looks as if it were a word of the family (*cf.* Luke ii. 19, 51). The expression " upon whom my name is called " (Acts xv. 17), is characteristic of James (Jas. ii. 7), as indeed is the use of " name " in this sense (*cf.* Acts xv. 14, 26, with Jas ii. 7, v. 10, 14). The word δαπανάω (Acts xxi. 24) used there probably by James, is used similarly in the Epistle (Jas. iv. 3), also the word for purify (Acts xxi. 24, *cf.* Jas. iv. 8). These and similar correspondences help to make us feel that we are all the time in contact with one and the same mind. The similarity of the word of greeting indeed in Epistle and Decree might suggest that the hand of the writer of the former was that of James himself.

Certain special features of the Epistle call now for consideration. (1) At the very least, tradition has attributed this writing to James the brother of the Lord because the early Church found in it just that type of mind which all the historical reminiscences of James, who held the place of authority in the Jerusalem Church for thirty years, declared him to be. The writer is an austere moralist, inclined to be very dubious of those who profess faith yet show little sign of it in their deeds. In varying ways he reiterates the words " Faith without works is dead." (Jas. ii. 14, 17, 18, 20, 22, 24, 26). It seems quite evident indeed that the writer is a Jewish Christian, a man firmly rooted in the ancient historic faith, yet no mere ceremonialist ; a man who firmly believes that the Gospel of Jesus has added a higher and more glorious illumination to the ancient religion. He calls Christianity " the engrafted word which is able to save your souls." And he summons men to obey not merely the Law of Moses, but what he calls " the perfect law of liberty " ; the " Royal Law," which he enunciates in the way Jesus did : " Thou shalt love thy neighbour as thyself." This description of the writer fits exactly the man depicted in these New Testament references we have considered.

(2) Perhaps the most marked feature of the letter has now to be considered. No one can read it without constantly coming across sayings and phrases which recall the great words and thoughts of Jesus. The Royal Law—" Love thy neighbour as thyself " (ii. 18)—reminds one of Jesus' emphasis on the two commandments on which hang all the Law and the prophets (Mark xii. 29), and of His own way of putting the golden rule : " Whatsoever ye would that others should do to you, do ye even so to them " (Matt. vii. 12).

Take again this writer's insistence on " works " as the proof of the reality of one's faith. Did Jesus never say anything like that ? This writer puts the thought in another way when he says " Be ye doers of the word, and not hearers only." And he proceeds to make a parable about the man who is a mere hearer and not a doer. Is there nothing like this in the end of the Sermon on the Mount ? " By their fruits ye shall know them." " Not every one that saith to me, ' Lord, Lord,' shall enter into the kingdom of heaven, but he that doeth the will of my Father." . . . " Whosoever heareth these sayings of mine and doeth them, I will liken him unto a wise man that built his house upon rock ; . . . . . And everyone that heareth these sayings of mine and doeth them not, shall be likened unto a foolish man that built his house upon sand . . ." (Matt. vii. 20f.). " Can men gather grapes of thorns or figs of thistles," said Jesus. Surely this writer is echoing that memorable word when he says : " Can the fig tree bear olive berries ? either a vine figs ? " (James iii. 12).

Then listen to this word from the Epistle : " Speak not evil one of another. . . . He that speaketh evil of his brother and judgeth his brother . . . judgeth (makes himself an administrator of) the law ; but if thou judge the law thou art not a doer of the law, but a judge. There is one law-giver, . . . who art thou that judgest ? " (iv. 11, 12). The writer simply means : it is the height of presumption to put yourself in the throne of judgment. By that very act you stand judged— and condemned, of censoriousness. Do we catch no echo of the thoughts of Jesus here—" Judge not, that ye be not judged " (Matt. vii. 1) ?

Or listen again to this from the Epistle : " He shall have judgment without mercy that showed no mercy " (ii. 13) ; and remember how Jesus said : " if ye forgive not men, neither will your Father forgive" (Matt. vi. 15). " Blessed are the merciful, for they shall obtain mercy " (Matt. v. 7). Remember His parable of the Unmerciful Servant.

Surely we find echoes of other beatitudes in this letter too. When the writer speaks of " the poor of this world, who are rich in faith and heirs of the kingdom " (ii. 5), is it not an echo of " Blessed are the poor in spirit, for theirs is the kingdom of heaven " (Matt. v. 3) ? When the letter-writer

says "the peacemakers who sow in peace reap
righteousness" (iii. 18), are we not reminded
of the blessedness of the peacemaker (Matt. v. 9) ?
When the writer says "count it all joy when
you fall into divers temptations" (i. 2), does it
not remind us of Jesus' words : "Blessed are
ye when men shall revile you and persecute you.
. . . Rejoice and be exceeding glad" (Matt.
v. 11) ? And when James goes on to say : "The
trying of your faith worketh patience. But let
patience have her perfect work that ye may be perfect
and entire, wanting nothing" (i. 3f.), and "we count
them happy who endure" (v. 11), do not the
words recall the good soil in the parable of the Sower :
"They who receive the word and keep it and bring
forth fruit with patience "(Luke viii. 15) ? Do they
not recall also that other word of Jesus : "In your
patience do ye enter into full possession of your
souls" (Luke xxi. 19) ?

Again, when James says : "Swear not, neither by
heaven, neither by the earth, neither by any other
oath : but let your yea be yea ; and your nay, nay
. . ." (v. 12), he is quite consciously and deliberately repeating a word of Jesus (Matt. v. 34-37).

Again, when James waxes vehement against riches,
is it not in perfect harmony with the teaching of
Jesus ? "Woe unto you rich ! . . How hardly shall
they that have riches enter into the kingdom ! . . .
The deceitfulness of riches !" said Jesus. "Go to,
ye rich men, weep, and howl !" says James (v. 1).
"Ye that say, To-day or to-morrow we will . . .
buy and sell—ye know not what shall be on the
morrow. For what is your life ? A vapour !"
(iv. 14). When we quote these words from James,
there rises before the mind Jesus' grim picture of

the man saying, " Soul, thou hast much goods laid up for many years. . . ." But God said : " Thou fool, this night thy soul shall be required of thee " (Luke xii. 16-21). " Your riches are corrupted, your garments are moth-eaten," says James (v. 2) ; and Jesus said : " Lay not up for yourselves treasures upon earth, where moth and rust doth corrupt . . ." (Matt. vi. 19). " The friendship of this world," says James, " is enmity with God. Whosoever therefore will be a friend of the world is the enemy of God " (iv. 4). " Ye cannot serve God and Mammon," said Jesus (Matt. vi. 24).

Or take the word about asking. " If any of you lack wisdom, let him ask of God, who giveth to all men liberally and upbraideth not : and it shall be given him " (Jas. i. 5). It is an echo of Jesus' word : " Ask and it shall be given. . . . Your heavenly Father knoweth how to give good gifts to them that ask Him " (Matt. vii. 7f.). " He maketh the sun to rise on the evil and the good, and sendeth rain on the just and the unjust " (Matt. vi. 45).

Again, " God resisteth the proud, but He giveth grace to the humble "—so James quotes an ancient scripture (iv. 6). It is a reflection of the very heart of Jesus' Gospel. " I thank thee, O Father, LORD of heaven and earth, because thou hast hid these things from the wise and prudent, and hast revealed them unto babes " (Matt. xi. 25). It is the little child who is greatest in the Kingdom ; it is the child who alone enters the Kingdom.

We might go on multiplying instances. The whole letter, in short, is saturated with the mind of Christ.

(3) But it is not merely the correspondence of thought and expression that we have to mark here.

We must note now the fact that the writer never expressly says that he is quoting Jesus, nor does he acknowledge any indebtedness to the Gospels. Indeed, hardly in any case can he be said to be quoting at all. We can, in fact, scarcely resist the conclusion that we are listening to the reproduction of thoughts from a mind that had lived and laboured for years alongside the Master-mind which created and gave them perfect utterance. They drop out freely and spontaneously, as from a mind that had so absorbed them that they had become part and parcel of its very self. Had James not listened to Jesus' talk, as they wrought side by side at the bench in Nazareth and Capernaum, and half-unconsciously, half-reluctantly, all his thinking had become moulded by it ? Perhaps the parables and pictures are Jesus' own.

More striking still, though he now writes as a believer in Jesus as Saviour and Lord, he does not even keep saying, " This was what Jesus thought." He nowhere says it at all. Is it not the natural delicacy of one who, being brother to Jesus according to the flesh, felt it might be boastful and vain to be always referring to " my brother," " my brother " ? It is in the very spirit of Jesus Himself. James would base no claim to authority on his consanguinity. Who was he to do that ? Jesus would not have liked it. The chief of his intimate memories of Jesus was far too sad, solemn, and tender for public gaze. And Jesus was far above him now, the Lord of Glory ; who was he to be always holding before men's eyes the fact that he was His kinsman according to the flesh ? It was honour enough for him to call himself His servant (Jas. i. 1).

Reserving for the moment a still more striking feature of the letter, surely already we can with a measure of confidence say that we feel behind this letter the mind, aye, and the heart of James the brother of Jesus. He was given the place of honour in the Jerusalem Church, because of his human relationship ; never once does he himself trade on this intimate connection.

IV

To this picture of James, tradition sets its crown and seal. The impression of the man which comes to us from beyond the bounds of Scripture, not only blends harmoniously with this, but carries the stamp of truth within itself. And it is a majestic and noble picture.

Hegesippus, the earliest historian of the Christian Church, himself a Christian Jew, has told the story of James in Jerusalem. James is to be distinguished from others of the same name, he tells us, by the title, " Just," a title which was applied to him from the first. " He was consecrated from his birth. He drank no wine nor strong drink. He ate no animal food. No razor ever touched his head. He did not anoint himself with oil or use the bath." This is the description of one whom the Jews would regard as a typically holy man. He was, as Clement puts it concisely in his *Recognitions*, an ascetic and a Nazirite.

James the Just !—it is a noble reputation to have won from all classes in Jerusalem. And it seems to have been the title given him not by Christians only, but by the whole population of Jerusalem. When the Jews wanted to describe one who came near to a perfect fulfilling of the Law, they called him " just and devout," and the words mean one who obeys the moral precepts in relation to one's fellow-men, and the ceremonial precepts in relation to God. But because James belonged to the sect of the Christians, orthodox Jews would not be so ready to call him " devout." There was no difference of opinion about the other title, however. By universal consent he was " the Just." His sensitive conscience in relation to moral principle made him universally respected. And even the Temple priests had little fault to find with him in his reverence for the ancient ceremonial.

This sheds a strong light not only on the nature of the Jerusalem Church, but on the Nazareth family as well. Not in the case of Jesus alone, but in the case of James, we see clear proof of a very careful upbringing. Nor were they exceptions in this home. It would seem that Judas and Simeon were marked religious men also. All the sons were named after great national leaders and patriarchs (Mark vi. 3). And the fact that James was a Nazirite means that his mother had taken this strict religious vow for him in infancy. Beyond a doubt this Nazareth home was one of the homes of the Chasidim—the pious in the land—the homes where the beating heart of the ancient faith could still be felt.

Now it was just to such homes that the sect of the Pharisees owed their origin. Since the *Book of Acts* informs us that a number of the Pharisees believed, and since we can without difficulty gather that they deferred to James' opinion, it is not improbable that James himself began his religious career as a Pharisee. To all intents and purposes at least it was a Pharisee believer that came to hold the position of authority for thirty years in the Church in Jerusalem. Here surely is a vivid searchlight flung on the obscurity of this early community. At first sight it seems astonishing that this growing and vigorous and disturbing new "Way," as it was called sometimes, should have held its place so long with comparative immunity from persecution, in the very stronghold of the Jewish faith. For in the last glimpse we get of it in *The Acts*, we hear what is probably the voice of James himself, speaking of the many thousands of Jews who believe. The fate of Stephen, who was the first to force into prominence the disruptive principles of Christianity, suggests, albeit by contrast, the line this Church took for itself. Nevertheless the New Way, for all the depression which it suffered in this incomplete version of it, was a standing menace and reproach to Israel. That "this sect" maintained its ground in the Holy City, therefore, must be attributed to the influence of James. For, according to the early and well accredited tradition, not only did the Temple priests acknowledge that he was a true and faithful Jew, but—so great was his reputation for sanctity—they allowed him, in spite of his Christian heresy, to enter the inner Temple, as though he were a priest or a Levite himself, and to join in the worship there. To quote Hegesippus again : "To him only was it permitted to enter the inner sanctuary." And then after telling of his constant vigil and atoning prayers in the Temple Courts he adds : "Through his exceeding righteousness he was named *Oblias* (*i.e.*, 'defence of the people ')." Thus through this extraordinary man, wholly given to the life of prayer, the clash between the Temple and the Church of the Christians in Jerusalem was prevented. So great a hold had the New Way taken of the city that strife between the new and the old would have meant a violent disruption of the city's life. Doubtless everyone felt this, and this was the reason for the name *Oblias*—the people's bulwark. Such a *régime* could not continue. It went down in blood at length, and Jewish Christianity succumbed to the disease which was inherent in it, and which only a holy life staved off so long. The liberation wrought by Stephen was a nobler achievement than the conservation effected by James. Yet James' task may have had its own part in the plan of God for His Kingdom.

V

And now at last we are in a position to disclose this man's story, which lies hidden in the New Testament, and to complete it with the aid of extra-canonical history. The tragedy of the Nazareth family was the tragedy of an estrangement; the glory of it was the reconciliation that brought this disunion to an end. It was a family in which the Eldest Born turned out to be a Youth of supreme religious insight, knowing His ancient faith as few knew it, loving His people's history as few loved it, and yet, because of His possession of a new and un-heard-of intimacy with God, convinced that the religious leaders of the day had blinded the people and led them astray—so convinced, so passionately convinced of it, that He became the greatest religious Reformer the world has ever known, nay more, the Supreme Instrument of God in the destiny of mankind. And on the other hand, there was the second son of the family, James—without the insight, the originality, the burning magnetic spirit of Jesus; but as deeply imbued in the ancient traditions and Law—narrow, conservative in his outlook, an ascetic glorying in the vow he was under, a Pharisee in spirit, perhaps even in name. It was inevitable that the two spirits should clash, and that James should grow bitter and censorious as he wrought beside Jesus at the bench. It seems likely that the family of brothers, the mother along with them, went from Nazareth to Capernaum after the baptism at the Jordan (John ii. 12). The word in John's Gospel seems a pure fact of history. Perhaps the business in Nazareth was surrendered to make a home for a married sister ; it was just after the marriage in Cana, and none of the sisters seem to have accompanied them (Mark vi. 3). A new business may have been opened in Capernaum; but they were not long there before Jesus began His Gospel campaigning. And in a few weeks the rupture of the family relations took place. Is there no evidence, no hint of this family unhappiness, in the talk of Jesus ? Did He not say in poignant irony once : " I am come to set a man at variance against his father, and the daughter against her mother, and the daughter-in-law against her mother-in-law. *And a man's foes shall be they of his own household* " ? Or listen again to these words. Do they not seem to come from the depths of a bitter sad experience ? " I say unto you, That whosoever is angry with his brother without a cause shall be in danger of the judgment ; and whosoever shall say to his brother Raca (Fool) shall be in danger of the council, but whosoever shall say Morê (Knave) shall be in danger of Gehenna fire. Therefore, if thou bring thy gift to the altar, and there rememberest that thy brother hath ought against thee, leave there thy gift before the altar and go thy way ; first be reconciled to thy brother, and then come and offer thy gift. . . ." Or this word : " So likewise shall my heavenly Father do also unto you, if ye from the heart forgive not every one his brother their trespasses." Or this revealing word spoken in His native town : " A prophet is not without honour save in his own country and *among his own kin and in his own house*" (Mark vi. 3f., *cf.* John vii. 3).

These words are the overflow of a heart that knew its own bitterness. But the story itself lies there, half hidden on the Gospel page. The brethren —for they were all in sympathy with James—began to resent His ongoings. Perhaps they were annoyed the day He chose the Twelve and brought them home to the house. The attempt to have a meal together was interrupted. The crowds had gathered. The scornful officials of the synagogue were muttering, " He is in league with the devil—it is the power of Beelzeboul." And the family doubts about the Elder Brother came to a head. Even His mother was influenced against Him. And they all appeared this day on the outskirts of the throng while He was passionately haranguing the people. Perhaps some cunning scribes had thought to end His reforming career, not merely by making insinuations about His sanity themselves, but by persuading the family to display their suspicions openly too. James, the second eldest, would be the primemover in this, and it would seem that Jesus heard James' excited voice saying : " We must take Him home—He is mad, He is mad—He is beside Himself " (Mark iii. 21). And one of the crowd said, " Here are your mother and brothers outside wanting you." No epigram, no maxim of cold philosophy; far more than indignant rebuke—the words that follow; every syllable of them is a drop of blood. "Who is my mother, and who are my brothers?" asked the quivering lips. Then He looked round—and round—on them which sat about Him (Mark iii. 34).

To quote words we have used elsewhere: " The memory of that look never faded out of Peter's mind. It is due to him, we have it recorded in the Gospel. Anguish, shame, yearning, sorrow unutterable; a long hesitation while the call of the blood, the love of family, the ties of home, tugged and strained at His heart. And then they broke. Thrusting out His hand (Matt. xii. 49)—the only time we are ever told of a gesture of the Master's hands while He spoke in public—in an abrupt, swift movement towards His twelve disciples, He said: 'Behold, my mother and my brethren! For whosoever shall do the will of God, the same is my brother and sister and mother.' That was enough. Mother and brethren understood, and turned and stole away. And as they went, His brother James, stung to alertness by the smart of the rebuke, caught the sad words like a knell of doom, 'I say unto you that every idle word that men shall speak, they shall give account thereof at the day of judgment' (Matt. xii. 36). James had called his Brother mad. An idle word! A cruel word, worse than the thrust of an assassin's sword! The last of many."

Is it merely fanciful to say that James heard his Brother's reproach in this word? We turn once more to the Epistle of James—to consider the point we deferred some pages back. And at once words leap to light which almost compel us to believe they come from this brother of the Lord. Let me repeat them here. "My beloved brethren, let every man be swift to hear, slow to speak, slow to wrath ; for the wrath of man worketh not the righteousness of God" (i. 19). Then a little later this : "If any man among you seem to be religious and bridle not his tongue, but deceiveth his own heart, this man's religion is vain" (i. 26). And later this : "If any man offend not in word, the same is a perfect man, and able also to bridle the whole body. . . . The tongue is a little member, and boasteth great things. Behold how great a matter a little fire kindleth ! And the tongue is a fire, a world of iniquity ; . . . it defileth the whole body, and setteth on fire the course of nature ; and it is set on fire of hell" (iii. 6).

And does not this read like a deliberate contrast between his own proud, Pharisaic, so-called wisdom and the wisdom of the meek and lowly One ? "If ye have bitter envying and strife in your hearts, glory not, and lie not against the truth. This wisdom descendeth not from above, but is earthly, sensual, devilish. For where envying and strife is, there is confusion and every evil work." What a picture of divided brotherhood that is ! "Wherever jealousy and rivalry exist, there disorder reigns, and all sorts of evil actions." But James knew well that the cause lay not at all with his Elder Brother— only with himself, his bitter and jealous self. For do not the words that follow read like James' veiled picture of the gentle Heart of Love that, many a time beside the bench, refused to be provoked by his bitter tongue : "But the wisdom that is from above is first pure, then peaceable, gentle, easy to be entreated, full of mercy and good fruits, without duplicity, straightforward. And the

peace-makers who sow in peace reap righteousness "
(Jas. iii. 14ff.) ?

As we listen to all these words, do they not convey
to us the feeling that they are the confession of one
who had too much reason to know the sin and sorrow
of a bitter tongue—the record in short of James'
belated remorse ? For in spite of the fact that he
refused to be convinced by Jesus in his early intercourse with Him, that he listened, with a hostile and
censorious heart, to the golden words dropping
from the gracious lips, surely this letter proves what a
deep impression those sayings of the Master made in
his mind. He could not get away from them. The
angry opposition of James to Jesus was simply the
explosive violence of a thoroughly unhappy man.

But why did Jesus repudiate His kinsfolk, sever
the ties of blood, renounce home ? Because it was
no longer home to Him, for one thing. Where
love ceases, home is no more. But chiefly it was in
the interests of a holier ideal of home. " Whoever
does the will of God, that is my brother and sister
and—mother." (" And mother ! "—the last words
to fall from His reluctant lips at this time ; it cost
Him the effort of a son's breaking heart). They who
do God's will—these were the ones who now claimed
the undivided love of His heart. So, in the very
moment when He made Himself homeless, He
constituted His new family, under the open sky.
He became homeless for the sake of the true ideal
of home—homeless that men might learn to take
God with them into their homes and make them
homes indeed.

And so it proved for the Nazareth family. When
the news reached Galilee that Jesus' life was in danger,
that He was in Jerusalem, and that any day He might

die, the memory of the gentle Soul so passionately convinced of the sweet mercy of God, and the thought of Him now steadfastly, consistently facing death for the sake of His convictions, overcame the hostile brother, and with the whole family he travelled south to Jerusalem (John xix. 25 ; Acts i. 14).

In terrible suspense the family waited, eagerly gleaning scraps of information about each stage of the trial. Then came the news of the sentence of death. And all James' long-crushed love for a noble brother broke through the hard crust of religious bigotry and pride. And all his bitter revilings of the early days in Nazareth and Capernaum rushed up before his eyes to condemn him. He had deceived his own heart. He had fancied he was religious— a very superior and self-righteous person he had been, but what about his tongue ? Had he always bridled his tongue ? Nay, it had been a spark of fire that had set all his soul ablaze as with the flames of hell. It had wrought estrangement, confusion, sorrow, tragedy, in the home. He had thought himself wise ! He had *lied* against the truth ! His wisdom was anything but from above. It was simply vain tradition, earthly wisdom, fleshly, devilish.

And over against that solemn self-conviction rose the noble form of the Brother he had wronged. So gentle, so silent, answering not again—true to Himself till the last in Caiaphas' judgment hall, so pure, so peaceful, so easily entreated, so full of compassion, so singlehearted. Yes, in a thousand ways He had shown by His life how infinitely He transcended him in goodness. There was absolutely no hypocrisy in Him—transparent through and through. It was all clear to James now ; Jesus was right and he was terribly wrong. With Him all the time was the wisdom that is from above. He would seek His forgiveness ere it was too late. And he hastened out. But the grim procession had passed on to Calvary. He followed almost beside himself with grief. But already the eyes were glazed in death. He could speak to Him nevermore.

He returned to Jerusalem dazed and dumb. They could not get him to speak or to break his fast. Three days passed like this. Then came news that Peter, who was in like case with himself, had found peace for his tormented soul—had been made aware of the Presence of Jesus—*risen from the dead*, and had felt the Divine forgiveness flowing into his torn heart from the living touch of his Lord. James listened in frenzied suspense. His rigid face relaxed. His whole frame was shaken in a paroxysm of grief and longing and despair. Then the words came— terrible, fierce, pitiless, unsparing of himself. " I have sworn a vow," he said, " that I would eat no bread from the hour I saw my Brother on the Cross ; never again will I eat bread, unless I see Him, unless He speaks to me from beyond the grave, unless I am permitted to speak my repentance to Him."

This tradition is recorded for us in *The Gospel according to the Hebrews*. And one can scarcely doubt that it is essentially true. His wish was granted. It befel him as it had befallen Peter. His crucified Brother came back to him ; how, we know not, but Paul tells us that it happened. The peace of a reconciliation, sweet yet terrible, took possession of James, and through him, it reached the rest of the family. He must have heard from Jesus' lips words like those the brothers heard from the long lost Joseph in Egypt centuries ago : " I am Jesus, your brother, whom you cast out from the home in Galilee. Now, therefore, be not grieved nor angry with yourselves. . . . God sent me forth from you to save lost lives, . . . to save them by a great deliverance. It was not you that sent me to the Cross, but Love—God."

Though it is only vaguely hinted at in the New Testament, it is one of the most thrilling and moving of all the instances of the power that was given to the Son of Man on earth to forgive sins. And the result of it travelled far. Through James' experience, doubtless, the mother and brethren were persuaded to wait with the little company in the Upper Room, until in answer to their long vigil of prayer and fasting, there came on them the great ecstasy of Pentecost. The Spirit of the risen Jesus took possession of their souls with contagious and resistless power. And James became a dedicated life—dedicated to the service of his Brother's Cause. Raised by universal consent to be head of the Church in Jerusalem, he made it the one aim and object of his life to atone for, and undo, the blood-curse which the Jewish people had deliberately taken on themselves by the Cross of Jesus. It was his desire to win Jerusalem, to win the nation, for the Kingdom. Reconciled to God by the Great Peacemaker, who had wrought reconciliation in the family by His death, he would now be a reconciler too. He stood between the rapidly growing Church in Jerusalem and the ancient hierarchy of the Temple, a life consecrated to this holy task. And he won the reverence and respect of both sides. He stopped many a fierce quarrel that might have led to bitter persecution and bloodshed. For the Roman guard looked on, ready to intervene and suppress rioting with a ruthless hand. Again and again the city had James to thank for preserving its peace. It was for this that he came to be called "Oblias"—bulwark of the people. Day after day he spent, praying on bended knees for the people's forgiveness—praying (the old tradition in the record of Hegesippus means) that the national sin, the tragic shame and curse of having reared the Cross, might be undone, and the whole race brought in, reconciled, won for the Gospel and the Kingdom of God ; praying—this ancient story goes on to say—until his knees became like camel's knees, padded with great, thick callosities of horny skin.

Then came the end. In the year 62 A.D.— according to Josephus the historian—during an interval between the death of Festus, before whom Paul was tried, and the arrival of his successor Albinus, the high Priest Anan, a rash, impulsive spirit, arrested James and delivered him—to be stoned. Jerusalem was at this time rapidly passing into that turbulent condition of anarchy and revolution which ended in the revolt from Rome, and the subsequent siege and fall of the city in 70 A.D. Here in this moment when the reins of Roman control were relaxed, the revolutionary party of the priests determined to suppress this new faith which was making rather for peace with Rome. Was it perhaps to the restraining hand of James, that Paul was referring, when he wrote to the church in Thessalonica : "The secret force of lawlessness is at work already ; only it cannot be revealed till he who at present restrains is removed" (2 Thes. ii. 7) ?

James was subjected to a semblance of a trial, like his brother Jesus. They enquired about the New Way. "O thou Just One," they asked, "to whom we are all bound to listen, what is the door of Jesus ? " The clue to the strange question lies in the Gospel of John, who was a member of the Jerusalem church up till this time. In that Gospel Jesus is represented as saying, " I am the Door ; by me if any man enter in he shall be saved." The " Door " was a familiar figure for expressing religious truth in the East. The Persians call their great mediator Bahu, " Bab " the Gate, to signify that his soul is the spiritual portal between the unseen world and the earth, and that believing in him means winning access to this spiritual or Divine world. So when they asked James this question they meant : " In what way does He claim to bring men into contact and communion with God ? " And James answered : " You ask me concerning Jesus the Son of Man ? He is both seated in heaven on the right hand of Power, and He will come again on the clouds of heaven."

These are familiar words repeating the great claim which Jesus made for Himself in the days of His flesh, and which is made for Him again and again in the *Book of Acts*. Translated into the thought of our day, it means : Jesus has been raised up from the dead. His human life, entering the realm of the Eternal beyond the grave, has not only been set free from its earthly limitations, but has been endowed with full control over the spiritual resources of God. Through His risen life the power of the Spirit now flows into the lives of the believers. James is therefore bearing testimony to Pentecost, and to every manifestation of the Spirit in the story of the spread of Christianity in those early years. But by that word, " He will come again on the clouds of heaven "—the way the dreamers spoke of the triumphant vindication of the Kingdom of God among men at last—James is declaring that this new Faith is going to have a world-wide victory, and to displace all older forms of faith.

And the crowd, listening in the court of the Sanhedrin, cried, "Glory to God!" And many believed. The scribes and Pharisees when they heard the shouting in response to James' answer, feared lest the people would look to Jesus, and they said, "We have done ill in bringing about such a testimony to Jesus. Alas! even 'the Just' has gone astray. Let us go up and cast him down." So James was led to a pinnacle of the Temple and flung down. Then they called on their hired assassins to stone him, for he was not killed outright by the fall. And James, kneeling in his martyr hour in the place where his Brother was condemned to death, followed in the footsteps of Him who had become his Saviour, as with his latest breath he prayed, "O Lord God my Father, I beseech thee forgive them, for they know not what they do." Then a fuller smote him on the head with his club. James' testimony was ended—and crowned. They buried him there; and on a monument to mark the spot, it is said his comrades inscribed: "He hath been a true witness both to Jews and Greeks that Jesus is Christ."

He had proved his faith by his life—his works. His works do follow him.

> And still unwavering faith holds sure
> The words that James wrote sternly down:
> Except we labour and endure
> We cannot win the heavenly crown.
>
> O Way Divine, through gloom and strife
> Bring us Thy Father's Face to see.
> O heavenly Truth, O precious Life,
> At last, at last, we rest in Thee.

CHAPTER XI

The Story of a Runaway Phrygian Slave

I

In the wild heart of Asia Minor, where the natives only felt an occasional faint and far-flung ripple from the tides of the Greek and Roman civilisation, which washed all the shores of the Mediterranean, and swept some way inland along the great roads of three Continents, stood the town of Colossæ, a little place of somewhat faded importance. Laodicea, the upstart city, only ten miles away, had robbed it of its commercial prosperity. And Hierapolis, near by, with the glamour of an ancient religion about its grey walls, stood for all that this wild superstitious people knew about God. Colossæ was situated on the Lycus, a tributary of the Mæander, at a point where the river passes through a narrow gorge between sheer and rocky banks. The water of the river is nauseous, and impregnated to a most unusual degree with carbonate of lime, which has formed very remarkable incrustations along its course. Rising steep from the valley in which the city lay, is Mount Cadmus, towering to a height of seven thousand feet. It is a wild scene, a torn, convulsed, uncanny landscape. It was the home of the earthquake, and in one visitation, a very few years after the date of our story, the city was destroyed. There amid the ruins lies buried the house round which is gathered much of the pathos and beauty of this tale. The story itself is immortal —something that neither time nor earthquake can destroy.

Like most small country towns, Colossæ had its comfortably-off, if not indeed wealthy families. Life had grown more leisurely in the place. And in that trembling, demon-haunted region, the minds of many turned to superstition, and of some to deep and serious thought. Rumours of the culture of Greece, which had found a home for itself away down in the city at the mouth of the long, winding Mæander, drifted up to this inland highland town. And the restlessness of youth found a direction for itself in the desire to dip into this speculative culture, for their own wild nature-religion did not satisfy the thoughtful minds.

Two youths in this city of Colossæ, the one " a lad of parts " though not, perhaps, of wealth, and the other a lad of wealth, thoughtful but not so gifted as his neighbour, became close friends, finding in each other kindred spirits, unburdening their hearts to each other on all the great questions of life, death, and the unseen spirit-world.

It came about that the two found their way to Ephesus, in course of time, to attend the lectures of a Sophist who had rather a reputation in that day—one Tyrannus. And here suddenly one day they found themselves in the midst of the most exciting and—as it proved—the most momentous episode of their lives. It was announced in the class-room that a certain Jew, professing a new and wonderful religion, was to give a course of addresses here, at 11 a.m. — as the Western Text of the *Book of Acts* (xix. 9) informs us—daily. They resolved to attend, and, almost before they were aware, they were caught in the spell created by the burning, eager, sincere, and terribly in earnest little man. These two young men were among the large and growing crowd that " found the light " under the preaching of the Apostle. For he wrote one of them a private letter afterwards in which he reminded him " you owe me your very soul " (Philem. 19). And when he wrote to the Church at Colossæ about the same time he called the other " our dear fellow-servant who is a faithful minister of Christ on *our* behalf " (Col. i. 7)—a word which shows that when he received the Gospel he received a Christian vocation also from Paul. There can be little doubt that the great day for both of them was during Paul's long residence in Ephesus, when " all who dwelt in Asia heard the word " (Acts xix. 10). How eagerly and continuously they must have talked over the great event, in their rooms. The wealthier of the two had a body-servant whom he brought with him to Ephesus, and this slave doubtless listened with a vague wondering curiosity to the excited, joyous talk of these two young men, and to their rapturous description of the strange, uncouth, little preacher, and his moving story of the human God who was done to death on a cross—His only crime being that He loved his fellow-men too well. Perhaps this slave had even seen the Christ-intoxicated Jew, for the young men had become his friends and he may have visited them in their rooms. But the dull ears of the Phrygian slave could not comprehend his talk. He was among those who were

> Bound who should conquer, slaves who should be kings,
> Hearing their one hope with an empty wonder,
> Sadly contented with the show of things.

II

By-and-by the time came for the two young men to return to Colossæ. And they went back as flaming propagandists of the new faith. The rich Philemon arranged a meeting in his house and invited all his friends and acquaintances. His humbler but more eloquent and learned friend did the talking (Col. i. 7). Indeed, Paul calls this Epaphras in the passage just referred to " my beloved fellow-slave." And in the private letter to his friend, " my fellow-captive," which is probably Paul's way of honouring him, or giving him a rank equal with his own. There is a tradition which Jerome mentions dubiously, that Epaphras and Paul were carried captive in war from Judæa to Tarsus, together. Possibly the difficulty of this word " fellow-captive " has suggested the tradition. It may be that Epaphras was sharing Paul's room with him in Rome at the time of writing, and in this sense he might be called a fellow-captive. But it is possible also that he is using the word in a metaphorical sense, and associating Epaphras with himself as among those carried captive in the triumph-march of the Nazarene. In any case it is clear from the words that Epaphras was the chief servant of the Church in Colossæ (Col. iv. 12), the one who brought the good news to Colossæ, for in one of the passages referred to, the best MSS. omit the word " also," which, if it were allowed to stand, would suggest that *Paul* had preached there too (*cf*. Col. iv. 12).

Their story was seed which fell on receptive soil. One of those who believed, a girl called Apphia, Philemon married. And another relative, a frequent inmate of Philemon's house, was Archippus, a brother

(or a son) (Philem. 2). The congregation of Colossæ
met in Philemon's house (*ibid.*). Not content
with starting the new religion in their own city,
Epaphras and Philemon went to Laodicea and
Hierapolis, and were the means of setting Christian
Churches going there (Col. vi. 13). Though
Paul, the apostle of the Gentiles, did not
found these churches, and was never, so far as we
know for certain, present in these towns prior to
the time of writing, unless just on a flying visit,
the fact that these two were won for Christ by Paul
is the reason why he can yet write letters to these
churches, and do it as one whose word had authority.
The two were converts of his own, and had been
urged by him to carry the message thither.
Epaphras, it would seem, had become a kind
of peripatetic evangelist in these towns, and
Archippus apparently looked after the congregation
in Colossæ while he was away (Col. iv. 17).

III

Our story, however, is not so much with these
men as with Philemon's Phrygian slave. This
poor barbarian who had evidently won his way
into the confidence of his master, and was trusted
by him, was one day given a responsible task to
execute which proved too great a temptation. And
he absconded—disappeared from Colossæ ; Philemon
lost him, and probably some of his money too
(Philem. 18). Doubtless a hue and cry was raised
and a search instituted. But it was too late. The
slave had got clean away, and no trace of him could
be found.

Yonder he goes on the dusty highway leading
down the valley of the Mæander, making for the

sea-coast, travelling along the only road he was acquainted with beyond the environs of Colossæ, avoiding fellow travellers, ever and anon glancing in terror behind him, deserting the road and lying low when horsemen, or camel-drivers pressing on in haste, seemed likely to overtake him; reaching Ephesus at length, dreadfully tired and sorry for himself, but afraid to go back; stealing down to the harbour and bargaining to work his passage on the first vessel he saw preparing to go; then out to sea at last, a poor, ignorant hill-bred youth who had hardly ever seen the sea, neither knowing nor caring what destination the ship was bound for. We cannot be very certain of the route he followed. Probably it was across to Cenchreæ, where he left the ship and walked over the isthmus to Corinth. There he may have tried for a time to get work among the dock-labourers. But he must have found himself still too much in touch with his old home. There were too many of his own countrymen, perhaps even some he knew, passing and repassing here, to make it comfortable for him. So he went to sea again and came at last to Italy and Rome.

Here in the greatest city of the known world, with all its teeming multitudes, and especially its vast crowds of slaves, it would be easier for him to lose himself and so make good his escape. But just because of that very vastness and indifference in which he thought to lose himself, he only came to himself, and found it was his own uneasy conscience he had been trying to run away from all the time. Wandering the streets of the capital alone, aimless and disconsolate, his conscience worrying him, memories of his master's kindness and trust working remorse, picking up a precarious living by doing odd jobs that no one else would do, hungry and thinking often of the abundant food provided for the bond-servants of his master, homesick and thoroughly wretched, he was, one imagines, taken pity on by some of his own kind—slaves even as he had been. For it is hardly possible that he could have come directly into contact with the prisoner Paul. Poor and miserable enough was the lot of these slaves, but none of them so poor as he who had so desperately snatched at his freedom. He marvelled much at their tenderness, until he found they were worshippers of the strange new God his master had begun to worship. Possibly they had invited him to attend some of their meetings down in the catacombs, the subterranean resting-places of the dead—weird surroundings surely for praise and prayer. He must have heard them talk of the great little man who had done so much to carry the Good News all over the eastern part of the empire, and who had said and done so much on behalf of their class, the slaves (1 Cor. vii. 21, 22 ; Eph. vi. 7, 9 ; Gal. iii. 28 ; Acts xvi. 18, etc.). And as bit by bit he listened to their description of the man, an old memory began to wake in him, and to knock sleepily just outside the threshold of his mind, clamouring for recognition. At last the door in that forsaken mental room opened —and he knew ! Yes, it was in Ephesus, in the rooms of his master, that he had seen this man. It was his master's old friend. It was Paul.

IV

A great hope flamed up suddenly in the slave's hungry heart. By hook or by crook he would find his way to Paul's prison cell. He had had enough of wretchedness and despair. It would ease his miserable heart to breathe out his confession into the ear of his master's old friend. So one day Paul was startled by this unlooked-for arrival in his cell. Paul wondered for a moment where he had seen the lad before. But as soon as the slave spoke, Paul knew. Kneeling at the Apostle's feet he told his confused and shamefaced tale.

In fancy we stand for a moment in the cell, listening to the voice of Paul. " And so," we hear him say, " you were tired of slavery and you wanted freedom. And now you have found that being the slave of a good master is ten thousand times more to be desired than a bad freedom. You are tired of freedom. Look at me ; I am like you, a slave— the fettered slave of Jesus Christ. . . ." In some such way Paul would make his opening (it was a familiar thought of his) ; and then to the poor wretch he would tell the tale he was never tired of telling—of Jesus Christ the Crucified. And before long, in that prison cell a Roman soldier looked on and wondered what was happening, while the angels of heaven looked on and rejoiced in the presence of God over another lost and wandering sheep brought home on the shoulders of that Good Shepherd, of whom the Christian slaves had tried to tell him, while they pointed to His picture on the walls of the catacombs.

And now this slave, who had snatched at freedom and found it bitter—far from home, out of work, down at heel, hungry, lonely, hungry for kindness most of all, became the willing slave of this bond-slave of Jesus Christ. There was something very lovable in the simple-minded Phrygian. Had not his master liked him and trusted him ? And Paul

grew to love him as a brother (Philem. 12, 16).
Very moving was the devotion of this spiritual son
whom God had sent to comfort him in the cramped
life of the Roman prison. No doubt he rallied
him sometimes very gently and tenderly
" Onesimus ? Do you mean to tell me your name
is ' Onesimus ' ? You know what it means ? It
means ' useful.' *You* were not very useful or profitable to your old master the day you ran away ! You
were not ' Onesimus ' that day. You lost your name.
You became Achrestus—' useless, unprofitable.'
But now I have found you, and you have become
' Useful ' again. Nay, I will give you a new name.
Euchrestus is your name—Profitable, Goodhelp,
. . ." And so the days passed by and the slave's
happiness grew ; and with it a haunting unhappiness. Paul saw it, planned it, worked for it.
It was to create that unhappiness that he talked so
much about Colossæ and Philemon—Onesimus'
old master.

V

Visitors came and went frequently in the
Apostle's cell. One day Onesimus found Paul
excited—greatly excited. And he said to the slave,
" I want you to stay beside me to-day, Onesimus. I
am expecting friends." By-and-by two men were
shown in, and Onesimus started and blenched when
he saw them. Men from Colossæ—one of them
his old master's greatest friend ! And he waited
trembling in the shadows of the room, hiding his
face from the strangers' gaze.

" Peace to thee, Tychicus, brother beloved, and
to thee, Epaphras, fellow-worker in Christ ! What
news from Ephesus and Colossæ ? "

There had been trouble in the Churches of the great valley. False teachers had appeared. In particular some men had come to Colossæ, and had begun to play upon the old superstitions of the Colossian Christians. They had talked about the demons who had haunted the land in that torn, dishevelled, earthquake-ridden place, demons that still laid upon them their old evil spell. They had begun subtly to decry the name of Christ. That name, they said was not a sufficient charm against the demons. He was but one Revealer among many. They must adopt and practise the old Jewish Law, mediated by the angels, the ancient religion of the people out of whom Christ came (Col. ii. 8, 15, 18 20ff.). All the old weary round of meats and drinks, holy-days, new moons and Sabbaths, they were to observe again. (Col. ii. 16). And some were being drawn away. Even Archippus, it would seem, was inclined to dabble with the strange doctrine (Col. iv. 17). Epaphras told his story sore at heart, and indeed in an agony of prayer (Col. iv. 12). For he saw all his work in danger of being undone. That was what had brought him this long, long journey to visit Paul. And now he was worn with travel, unable for the immediate return journey. But Tychicus was ready to go back if only Paul would write a letter to the little church to help them to fight these insidious false teachers, especially the man who was making such a deep impression on the Colossian Christians by his show of wisdom (Col. ii. 9). And Epaphras began to speak in love, and pity, and longing affection, of his dear friend Philemon, who was bravely holding to the faith, as he had learned it of Paul in Ephesus.

A Runaway Phrygian Slave

Lost in intimate talk, absorbed in deep concern over the situation, they had forgotten they were not alone. But here they were interrupted. We fancy that Onesimus the slave had crept nearer and nearer, listening with mouth agape, all eyes and ears, to the moving story from his old home—till all the old memories awoke in him, and kneeling again, weeping, he now revealed himself to Epaphras, and unburdened his heart of all its unhappiness, of his longing to be reconciled to his master, to return, and be forgiven, and be to him as if the past had never been. " Onesimus," we seem to hear Paul saying, " this is what I have been waiting for. You will go back with Tychicus, and I will write a letter to your old master, which will make it all right between him and you. You will be restored, your transgression forgiven, the disgrace undone, and your life quite mended up again."

VI

The letter is here in the New Testament. It has no doctrinal importance, and in the early days was in danger of being left out of the Canon. What a tragedy that would have been! Something precious lost forever to the world. It is a letter " full of grace and wit " ; one of the most Christian documents ever penned. As a lesson in Christian tact and courtesy, in tender winsomeness, this letter, which lies enshrined like a sacred gem in the heart of the New Testament, will repay our closest study. It is, as Renan says, " A veritable little masterpiece in the art of letter-writing."

Let us put it into modern dress, pausing to note the charms and delicacies of it as we go along.

"Paul, the fettered slave of Jesus Christ, is writing this with the help of brother Timothy, to Philemon the beloved, our fellow-worker, to sister Apphia, to Archippus, our comrade-in-arms, to greet them, and the community that meets in your house; God our Father's love to you and peace, yes, and the Lord Jesus Christ's blessing too.

"I am constantly thanking my God, when I mention you in my prayers, since I am hearing of the love and the loyalty which you have toward the Lord Jesus and for all God's folk. And my confident prayer is that sharing the comradeship of your loyalty may result for them in an (equally) delicate discernment of the right thing for us Christians to do in every situation. For I have found great joy and comfort over your love, my brother; the open heart and open house you keep for every brother in Christ who knocks at your door."

What a rare skill the commencement of this letter shows! He mentions in general terms the fine reputation which Philemon has won for brotherliness, for hospitality. He puts Philemon on good terms with himself before he proceeds. He begins by calling himself "the bondsman of Christ"; and then he calls Philemon "brother." As much as to say "You are not ashamed to call this bondsman 'brother'; the comradeship of faith lifts you far above mere outward material status. You can recognise a brother in the soul of a slave who has believed in Christ. And after all what is any of us but a slave, a slave of Christ? That slavery lifts us into a region where the mere social status of an earthly slavery is forgotten, or ignored."

A Runaway Phrygian Slave

But that reference to Philemon's hospitality has a more subtle intention still. He puts it in the forefront of the letter, because he is going to lay on Philemon's hospitality the greatest strain he could possibly lay. " This is a letter to introduce a wandering believer," he in effect says. " God be thanked for your well-known hospitality ! Will you take him in and treat him with your usual kindness ? " Christian hospitality is not merely entertaining those of one's own social set, one's equals, everyday associates ; it is entertaining those who believe in the same God and Saviour, whether they be high or low, rich or poor, Jew or Greek, barbarian, Scythian, bond, or free. This is what the Cross of Christ does for a man. It makes his heart like the heart of God. And the anguish of the strain Paul is about to lay on Philemon goes very deep. It is an act of forgiveness he is about to ask him to perform. By a stroke of genius Paul translates forgiveness into hospitality. God's hospitality ! Is not the very spirit of hospitality part of the spirit which characterises the great, receptive, roomy, forgiving, heart of God ? But let us return to the letter. Paul goes on breaking his purpose to Philemon gradually, step by step. He has a request to make to him, but not till he comes to the seventeenth verse (in our Bibles) does he really state what it is :

" (Because of this well-known hospitality of yours, Philemon), I am making an appeal to you on the ground of love—although of course in Christ I should have no hesitation in enjoining you to do the fitting thing. It is I, Paul, the old man who make it (one of the grave and reverend seniors, as you will permit

me to call myself), aye, and a prisoner in chains
for Jesus Christ's sake. And my appeal to you
is on behalf of my spiritual son, born to me
while in chains."

He lingers to describe the man before mentioning
the name. We can almost fancy that Paul at the
very moment of writing is looking forward and
watching Philemon's face as he reads the letter.
And looking through Paul's eyes, we can see
Philemon's face brightening as he reaches these lines.
" O, this is going to be an easy request," Philemon
says to himself. " Paul wants me to do a good turn
to some new convert of his who is coming my way."
And then just at this point in the letter down
goes the name :

" It is Onesimus ! "

Then—as if he sees in spirit a little cloud gathering
on Philemon's brow—with a swift play upon the
meaning of the name, Paul seeks to scatter the cloud
before it grows menacing.

" ' Useful ' turned out anything but ' Profitable ' to you in former days, but to-day he has
become—true to his name—' Right-profitable '
to you—and to me also. Yes, to me ! I would
fain have kept him ; it is a sacrifice to let him
go. I am sending you my very heart. (What
a tender description of a slave !) I say I would
fain have kept him ('εβουλόμην—my inclinations
kept tugging one way) in order that, as your
deputy, he might be a house-slave to me in my
gospel bonds. But ('ηθέλησα—my will stepped in
and abruptly ended the struggle) I resolved not
to do anything without your approval, so that
your goodness to me might come of your own

free will, rather than under any pressure, so to speak.

"Perhaps this was the reason that you and he were parted for a while (" were separated!" What a gentle euphemism for absconding! Paul suggests that there was even a certain Providence—something of God—in the act), in order that you might get him back for always, no longer a mere slave, but something better than a slave—a brother beloved. A brother beloved, did I say? He is emphatically that to me. But how much more than emphatically so to you, both as fellow-man and a fellow Christian!" (Henceforth, Paul suggests, I shall only enjoy this brotherhood *in the Lord*, you will have him in the flesh as well as in the Lord.) "If then you recognise that fellowship (which I mentioned at the beginning),"—Paul here recalls his description of Philemon at the outset, as one willing to recognise him, the bondsman, as a brother,—" (here is my request at last.) Will you not take him back—as you would take me—myself? . . .

"(Is there a little difficulty still in the way?) Has he defrauded you? Have you a debt against him (for something that he took from you)? Put it to my account. Here is an I.O.U. for the amount : I PAUL, WILL REPAY— SIGNED BY MY OWN HAND! Although, talking of debts, I might have said, Charge it against yourself ; do you not owe me your own soul? Aye, brother, let me have ' profit ' of you— not materially, but in the Lord. (A reiteration of his previous witticism over the slave's name here.) Come, refresh my heart in Christ."

Then comes just a little hint that behind all this tender, sparkling, friendly pleading there lies the word of earnest authority; he means what he says.

"Relying on your *obedience*, I have written in this strain. I know you will do far more than I say.

"Now that is all for the present. Well, one thing more. See that you have the guest-room ready for me! I know that you are praying for my release—you all are. Surely your prayers will be answered soon.

"Epaphras, my fellow-prisoner in Christ, wants to be remembered to you. Mark sends his greetings, also Aristarchus, Demas, and Luke, my fellow-workers. May the love of our Lord Jesus Christ be with the spirit of all of you. Farewell."

VII

And so in the company of Tychicus, and bearing this precious letter, Onesimus set out for home, the prodigal returning from the "far country." He lingered shyly at the gate while Tychicus went in with the letter. Philemon read the letter, and a pleased look at once began to come into his face. By-and-by he broke out into laughter; and then he read on silently, but his lips trembled; he was moved. And when the reading was done, he sent for the fugitive and kissed him; and said: "Onesimus, you were my bondsman; you absconded and deserve to die. But you *have* died. You have escaped into another life, into another service—the service of Jesus. Henceforth you are free. You can stay if you like, but not as a slave any more. You must be one of

ourselves." Do not the *Apostolic Canons* tell of
this ? And tradition has it that Onesimus became
a bishop by and by. The city of Colossæ was laid
in ruins by an earthquake shortly after his return
home, but he at least escaped, bearing no doubt
the precious letter that obtained for him his pardon
and his ransom ; and also the letter to the Church
of Colossæ. Through this slave's gratitude, these
have been preserved for the Church of Christ as
priceless treasures never to be lost. " Of no
doctrinal importance " some of the early Fathers
thought this letter! Surely it is an Idyll of the
Grace of God. " We are all by nature *Onesimi*,"
says Luther.

BIBLIOGRAPHY

The books used in this work are classed for convenience under the different chapters. But certain books of general reference may be mentioned first.

GENERAL

The New Testament Writings.
Commentaries on the various New Testament Books.
Hastings' *Dictionary of the Bible.*
Hastings' *Dictionary of Christ and the Gospels.*
Hastings' *Dictionary of the Apostolic Church.*
Encyclopædia Biblica.

CHAPTER I

Nutt : *Studies on the Legend of the Holy Grail.*
T. A. Archer and W. L. Kingsford : *The Crusades.*
Josephus' *Antiquitates Judaicæ.*
Schürer : *The Jewish People.*
Stephen Graham : *The Priest of the Ideal.*

CHAPTER II

Sanday : *Sacred Sites.*
Edersheim : *Life and Times of Jesus the Messiah.*

CHAPTER III

David Smith : *Life and Letters of St. Paul.*
Zeller : *Stoics, Epicureans and Sceptics.*
W. L. Davidson : *The Stoic Creed.*

CHAPTER IV

W. B. Bacon : *Biblical and Semitic Studies.*
Skrine : *The Survival of Jesus.*

BIBLIOGRAPHY

CHAPTER V

J. B. Lightfoot : *The Brethren of the Lord* (in *Galatians*.)
Clement Alex. : *Pædagogus.*
Eusebius : *Historia Ecclesiastica.*
(*Talmud*.)

CHAPTER VI

Sir W. M. Ramsay : *St. Paul the Traveller and the Roman Citizen.*
David Smith : *Life and Letters of St. Paul.*
(Origen : *Homilies.*)

CHAPTER VII

Eusebius (*op. cit.*)
Josephus (*op. cit.*)
(*Talmud*.)

CHAPTER VIII

A. B. Davidson : *" Hebrews."*
A. S. Peake : *Introduction to the New Testament.*

CHAPTER IX

J. B. Lightfoot : *Cæsar's Household* (in *Philippians*.)
Suetonius : *Claudius.*
Shepherd of Hermas.

CHAPTER X

Clem. Al. *Recognitions.*
Hegesippus (quoted in Eus. *op. cit.*)
Josephus (*op. cit.*)

CHAPTER XI

Epistle of Paul to *Philemon.*
Epistle of Paul to *Colossae.*
Lightfoot : *On Colossians and Philemon.*
Erich Haupt : *Die Briefe an die Kolosser u. a. Philemon.*

INDEX OF NAMES, ETC.

Index

Index

Headley Bros., Ashford, Kent, & 18 Devonshire St., E.C.2.